US SUPREME COURT LANDMARK CASES

SLAVERY AND CITIZENSHIP
The Dred Scott Case

D. J. HERDA

Enslow Publishing
101 W. 23rd Street
Suite 240
New York, NY 10011
USA
enslow.com

YA
342.7308
HER

Published in 2017 by Enslow Publishing, LLC.
101 W. 23rd Street, Suite 240, New York, NY 10011

Library of Congress Cataloging-in-Publication Data

Names: Herda, D. J., 1948–, author
Title: Slavery and citizenship : the Dred Scott case / D. J. Herda.
Description: New York : Enslow Publishing, 2017. | Series: US Supreme Court landmark cases | Includes bibliographical references and index.
Identifiers: LCCN 2016032322 | ISBN 9780766084261 (library bound)
Subjects: LCSH: Scott, Dred, 1809-1858—Trials, litigation, etc.—Juvenile literature. | Slavery—Law and legislation—United States—History—Juvenile literature. | Slavery—United States—Legal status of slaves in free states—History—Juvenile literature. | United States—Race relations—History—Juvenile literature. | Scott, Dred, 1809-1858—Juvenile literature. | Scott, Harriet, approximately 1820-1876—Juvenile literature. | Lincoln, Abraham, 1809-1865—Juvenile literature. | Slavery—Law and legislation—Juvenile literature.
Classification: LCC KF228.S27 H475 2017 | DDC 342.7308/7—dc22
LC record available at https://lccn.loc.gov/2016032322

Printed in Malaysia

Portions of this book originally appeared in the book *The Dred Scott Case: Slavery and Citizenship, Revised Edition*.

Photo Credits: Cover, p. 32 © Dennis MacDonald/Alamy Stock Photo; p. 4 © Collection of the New-York Historical Society, USA/Bridgeman Images; p. 11 Chicago History Museum/Archive Photos/Getty Images; pp. 16, 52 Everett Historical/Shutterstock.com; p. 18 © North Wind Picture Archives; p. 21 © North Wind Picture Archives/Alamy Stock Photo; pp. 39, 43, 46, 55, 63 70, 82 Library of Congress Prints and Photographs Division; p. 73 Eddie Brady/Getty Images; pp. 75, 90 MPI/Archive Photos/Getty Images.

Contents

CHAPTER 1

Dred and Harriet—Free or Slave?

D red Scott huddled with his daughter Eliza while his wife, Harriet, gathered the last of their meager possessions outside their home in Fort Snelling, Minnesota—part of the sprawling vast Wisconsin Territory in 1840. As Harriet looked back at the building that had been their home for the past two years, she began to cry. She climbed into the wagon that would carry them to a steamboat bound south along the mighty Mississippi River. Soon, they would be back once more in St. Louis, Missouri.

Once their second daughter, Lizzie, had climbed aboard, Scott handed the infant to his wife before preparing to load the last of their belongings. Suddenly he caught sight of Harriet's tears.

Dred Scott lived from about 1799 until September 17, 1858.
He and his wife sued for their freedom in what came to be known as
the "*Dred Scott* decision."

He smiled and patted her hand. He knew they were not tears of sadness. They were tears of joy. The Scotts were finally going home.[1]

"Come along now," Dr. John Emerson called. "No time for that. We've a long trip ahead of us."

"Yes-suh," Scott replied. "Yes-suh, we sure do." Scott helped his wife aboard, and then he climbed in after her. As the couple settled down with their daughters, Emerson gave the order to move out, and the wagon lurched forward.[2]

It was spring, 1840, in Fort Snelling. Scott had accompanied Emerson, an army physician, from Missouri two years earlier. While in the North, Scott had met and married Harriet. Now they were returning home to St. Louis. Not to their home, but to Emerson's home: Scott, his wife, and their daughters were slaves.

Slavery was still an important part of the economy of the South in 1840. Slavery had long been banned north of a line roughly equal to the southern boundary of the state of Missouri. But Congress, in passing the Missouri Compromise of 1820–1821, had created a special exemption for that state, allowing Missouri to retain slavery.

The issue nonetheless remained a thorn in the side of northern political leaders, who saw slavery as an immoral and shameful institution. Southern leaders, on the other hand, needed inexpensive slave labor to help run their sprawling cotton, tobacco, and rice plantations.[3]

By 1840, the debate over slavery had mostly died down. But Dred Scott was destined to change all that.

He was destined to change his own future and that of his country, too.

Born a Slave

Dred Scott had been born in Virginia around 1800. The exact date was never recorded—not an unusual circumstance for the birth of slaves. He was the property of Peter Blow, a Virginia farmer. In 1818, Blow sold his 860 acres and moved with his family and slaves to a cotton plantation near Huntsville, Alabama. Two years later, Blow moved again, this time to nearby Florence, Alabama. Finally, in 1830, he settled for good in the bustling Missouri riverfront town of St. Louis, "the gateway to the West," on the mighty Mississippi River.

In St. Louis, the Blow family had to adapt to a completely different lifestyle. Rural Virginia and Alabama had been mostly cotton-growing country. But St. Louis, with its excellent port facilities, was geared more toward commerce, trade, and manufacturing. Blow rented a large home for twenty-five dollars a month and opened a boarding house, which he named the Jefferson Hotel. There, Dred Scott and the other Blow slaves worked—not in the fields, planting and hoeing and picking cotton, but in the hotel, cleaning and cooking, and running errands. It was quite a change for Scott, who had never known anything besides farming.

In 1831, tragedy struck the Blow family when Peter Blow's wife, Elizabeth, died. Early the next year, Blow sold the hotel and moved his family into another house. In the months that followed, Blow's own health failed, and he died on June 23, 1832, leaving the family fortunes in the hands of his eleven children.[4] Although no records exist of Scott's activities during the next few years, Scott himself once referred to the Blow children as "them boys" with whom he had been "raised." From this, it seems likely that Scott had been not only a slave, but also a good friend of the Blow family, especially the third son, Taylor, who would remain a lifelong supporter of Scott.[5]

Although no records have been found, Blow apparently sold Dred Scott to Dr. John Emerson, a St. Louis physician, who was about the same age as Scott. Emerson had moved to St. Louis in 1831 and had quickly befriended such well-known local figures as Missouri's US Senators Thomas Hart Benton and Alexander Buckner. He was also a friend of Dr. William Carr Lane, the first mayor of St. Louis; William H. Ashley, a Missouri congressman; and several members of the Missouri state legislature. Indeed, Emerson seems to have been better suited to making influential friends than practicing medicine, a profession in which he apparently was poorly trained and only minimally effective.[6]

Moving to Fort Armstrong

Nonetheless, on October 25, 1833, Emerson, who had applied for a position with the US Army, was accepted into the armed forces and appointed to the position of assistant surgeon. It was surely not his skill alone that got him the appointment.

After trying to gain a commission for years, it looked as if he would be passed over once again. But Emerson asked some of his most influential friends to come to his aid. Thirteen members of the Missouri state legislature signed a letter recommending him, as did Senator Benton. The following month, Emerson received his orders and moved to Fort Armstrong, on Rock Island, Illinois, taking Scott with him. Emerson reported to his commander, Lieutenant-Colonel William Davenport, and began what would eventually become a nine-year military career.

But life at Fort Armstrong proved less than comfortable. The fort's old log buildings were rotted and falling apart, and the roofs of the soldiers' barracks leaked with every rain. Undoubtedly, the slave quarters were worse. Despite frequent outbreaks of cholera and other diseases, Scott remained at Emerson's side, "in service" to the physician "as a slave and used by him as such."[7] In fact, Illinois had prohibited slavery since 1787, when the Congress of the Confederation passed the Northwest Ordinance, which banned slavery in the region. Based upon that, Scott could have sued for his freedom on the grounds that he was living in a free territory. For some reason, he did not. Instead, he stayed at his master's side.

Meanwhile, Emerson was unhappy with life on the plains. Within two months of his arrival at Fort Armstrong, he asked his commander for a leave of absence, claiming that he had contracted a "syphiloid disease" during a visit to Philadelphia. When his leave request was denied, Emerson once again enlisted his friends to pressure the War Department to transfer him back to St. Louis. Emerson himself informed the department that his left foot had developed a "slight disease" that might require surgery. In January 1836, he again requested reassignment, complaining that he had had an argument with one of his company commanders and could no longer work for the man.[8]

Despite his dissatisfaction with his position, Emerson did reap some rewards from his assignment. He bought several acres of land near the fort, along with an entire section across the Mississippi River, near present-day Davenport, Iowa. There, Emerson had Scott build a small cabin.

Finally, the War Department decided to close Fort Armstrong, mostly because of the poor condition of the fort. The fort, the government had decided, simply wasn't capable of protecting the residents of the area in light of the increasing hostilities with the American Indian tribes along the western frontier.

On to Fort Snelling

On May 4, 1836, after receiving his reassignment orders, Emerson and Scott moved, but not to St. Louis. Instead, Emerson had been ordered to Fort Snelling, some two hundred miles to the north, in the recently created Wisconsin Territory near present-day Saint Paul, Minnesota. Set on the west bank of the Mississippi, Fort Snelling was located in a portion of the Louisiana Purchase where slavery had been banned by the Missouri Compromise of 1820–1821. Once again, Scott could

DRED SCOTT. PHOTOGRAPHED BY FITZGIBBON, OF ST. LOUIS.

HIS WIFE, HARRIET, PHOTOGRAPHED BY FITZGIBBON, OF ST. LOUIS.

Harriet and Dred Scott are pictured here in an engraving from 1857. The image was printed in *Frank Leslie's Illustrated Newspaper,* published in New York.

have sued for his freedom, but he failed to do so. Instead, he remained in the service of Emerson, apparently never asking for his release from bondage.[9]

Shortly after arriving at Fort Snelling, Dred Scott's life was destined to change. There he met Major Lawrence Taliaferro, who worked at the Indian Agency near the fort. Taliaferro periodically left the territory to visit friends and relatives in Virginia, often returning with slaves whom he hired out or put to work in the agency. One of these slaves was Harriet Robinson, a teenager. Dred Scott and Harriet soon became good friends. In time, they married, despite the fact that Scott was more than twice her age.

Following the ceremony, a rare event for slaves, Taliaferro either gave or sold Harriet to Dr. Emerson. For the next several months, the two slaves worked for Emerson or whomever Emerson hired them out to. Following their first winter in the North, Emerson once again was hard at work petitioning the Surgeon General for reassignment, writing that the cold weather had "crippled him with rheumatism." He requested either a transfer to St. Louis or a six-month leave beginning the following autumn, barely in time to avoid another harsh winter.[10] This time, his request fell on receptive ears; and on October 20, 1837, Emerson was ordered to Jefferson Barracks near St. Louis.

More Changes

Emerson was elated with his new orders and quickly arranged for a canoe to take him part of the way south, where he could catch a steamboat to St. Louis. He was forced to leave behind most of his belongings and both of his slaves, all of which he planned to send for later.

But when Emerson arrived in St. Louis, he received bad news. His assignment had been changed, and he was now being ordered to Fort Jesup in western Louisiana.

Emerson arrived at Fort Jesup on November 22, 1837. Within two days, he had decided he hated swampy Louisiana even more than frigid Minnesota and wrote a request for transfer back to Fort Snelling, which, by comparison, suddenly looked good to him. Over the next few weeks, the doctor wrote several more letters explaining the undue hardships he was forced to endure in Louisiana. The damp climate had revived an old liver disorder, he claimed. Rheumatism had reared its ugly head and was causing him difficulty in breathing.

Despite his weakened physical condition, Emerson somehow managed to find the strength to pursue a whirlwind courtship, and he married twenty-three-year-old Eliza Irene Sanford (known as Irene), some fifteen years his junior. On February 6, 1838, shortly after the ceremony, Emerson sent for Dred and Harriet Scott to join his wife and him in Louisiana.

Following his honeymoon, Emerson again tried to get transferred from Fort Jesup. Once again, the Surgeon General gave in to Emerson's badgering, possibly hoping to end once and for all the stream of letters pouring onto his desk.[11] That September, Emerson was transferred back to Fort Snelling. After a brief stopover in St. Louis, the Emersons and their slaves boarded the steam-powered paddle wheeler *Gipsy* for the trip north. Another passenger on board, a Methodist missionary, later recalled in his memoirs, "Among the passengers were Dr. Emerson and his wife, having with them their servants, Dred Scott and his family, who belonged to this lady. On the upward trip one of Dred's children, a girl, was born."[12] Eliza Scott had been born in free territory north of the Missouri state line.

Emerson remained at Fort Snelling for two years until the outbreak of fighting with the Seminole Indians prompted his transfer to Florida in the spring of 1840. On the way to Cedar Key, Florida, Emerson dropped off his wife and slaves in St. Louis, where he felt they would be safe. Emerson served as a medical officer in the Seminole Wars for more than two years. During that time he sent repeated letters to the Surgeon General, complaining of recurring fever and other illnesses and requesting a transfer north. *Anywhere* north. Finally, with the end of the war, the Surgeon General, taking advantage of an order to reduce the size of the army's medical staff, gave Emerson an honorable discharge. Emerson suddenly found himself back in civilian life.

Following the discharge, Emerson's life took a turn for the worse. Unable to succeed in private medical practice in St. Louis, he decided to move with his wife to Davenport in Iowa Territory. There he opened a private practice, bought two city lots, and began building a brick house. By then his wife was expecting a child. But Emerson's health soon began to fail, and he died at the age of forty, just one month after the birth of his daughter, Henrietta.

Emerson willed all of his property to his wife, Irene. Mrs. Emerson had little need for slaves herself; so she hired out Dred and Harriet to her brother-in-law, Captain Henry Bainbridge, who kept the Scotts in his service until March 1846. He apparently took Dred Scott with him to Texas. Upon their return, Scott tried to purchase freedom for himself and his family, but Mrs. Emerson refused, hiring them out next to a St. Louis man named Samuel Russell, a wholesale grocer.

The following month, on April 6, 1846, attorney Francis B. Murdoch, on behalf of his clients Dred and Harriet Scott, filed petitions in the Missouri Circuit Court, outlining their former residence on free soil and requesting permission to file suit against Irene Emerson to establish their right to freedom. The judge granted them the right to sue, and, on that very same day, the Scotts filed actions for assault and false imprisonment. Dred's complaint stated that, on April 4, 1846, Mrs. Emerson had "beat, bruised and ill-treated" him and had imprisoned him for twelve hours. The complaint also stated that Dred was entitled to be considered a "free person" who had been held in slavery by the defendant, Mrs. Emerson. It claimed damages of ten dollars.[13]

After living for nearly half a century as a slave, Dred Scott had finally taken the first steps toward freedom. It would be a turning point in his life. But the suit would eventually turn out to be much larger than that of one slave and his wife seeking their freedom. It would soon become the rallying point of a nation, and the beginning of one of the most violent eras in American history.

CHAPTER 2

A History of Slavery

T he United States in the 1840s had undergone many changes since the earliest days of slavery. From the introduction of the first slaves in the colonies in 1619, the colonies had then gone through the Revolutionary War, becoming their own nation, and the War of 1812, proving they would fight to retain this new freedom. One thing, though, had not changed in the nearly two centuries prior to Dred Scott's birth—the South's ravenous hunger for slaves.

To those living in the North, southern slavery seemed a relatively simple answer to an economic problem. It was a way of life. While most northerners did not approve of slavery on moral principle, they nonetheless grudgingly acknowledged a need for its existence.[1]

This nineteenth-century engraving depicts twenty African slaves arriving in Jamestown in 1619.

This image shows slaves working a southern cotton plantation. Slaves were used for all parts of the process, from harvesting to baling to ginning the cotton.

To white southern slave owners, slavery was both an answer to the question of where to obtain cheap labor to work the cotton, rice, and tobacco fields and a complex socioeconomic structure upon which the Southern States based their very existence.

The entire southern way of life depended upon the sweat and toil of enslaved black workers. One South Carolina planter summed up the feelings of his countrymen this way: "Slavery with us is no abstraction but a great and vital fact. Without it our every comfort would be taken from us. Our wives, our children made unhappy—education, the light of knowledge— all, all lost and our people ruined forever."[2]

A Time of Expansion

As time passed and the institution of slavery became a common part of southern life, America began to grow from a relatively small community of people concentrated along the eastern seaboard to a rapidly expanding nation destined to settle the land from ocean to ocean. Following the Louisiana Purchase in 1803, French Americans in New Orleans began moving up the Mississippi River to St. Louis and from there into the lowlands of present-day Missouri. They were soon joined by pioneers and farmers from Ohio and Pennsylvania, and the region's population grew rapidly. By 1819, Missouri had attracted so many people that it was able to apply for admission into the Union as a state.

But the state constitution that Missouri submitted for approval to Congress permitted slavery. That set off a heated debate between southern pro-slavery and northern anti-slavery forces. The northern states had long since banned the buying and selling of slaves, and most had gone so far as to prohibit slavery with amendments to their state constitutions.

Missouri's request to enter the Union as a slave state posed a serious problem to Congress. Dozens of new states were yet to be formed from the land acquired by America in the Louisiana Purchase, as well as that in the sprawling Northwest Territory. Would these future states seeking to enter the Union be slave states or free? The answer to that could affect the decisions in Congress for years, decades, or even longer. In 1819, the number of free and slave states stood tied at eleven, providing political balance in Congress. No one group of politicians, pro-slavery or anti-slavery, had a majority vote in the Senate.

But when Missouri applied to enter the Union as a slave state, representatives of the northern free states objected. Admitting Missouri to the Union as a slave state would give the pro-slavery South a senatorial majority. That would provide southerners with enough votes to pass laws favorable to the South and unfavorable to the abolitionist North. Somehow, the ticklish question of slavery and the admission of new states to the Union had to be addressed.

In 1820, Speaker of the House Henry Clay came up with a solution to the problem by offering Congress a compromise. Clay proposed that a line be drawn westward from Missouri's southern border through the recently acquired Louisiana Territory. All territories north of that line were free to form states in which slavery was prohibited,

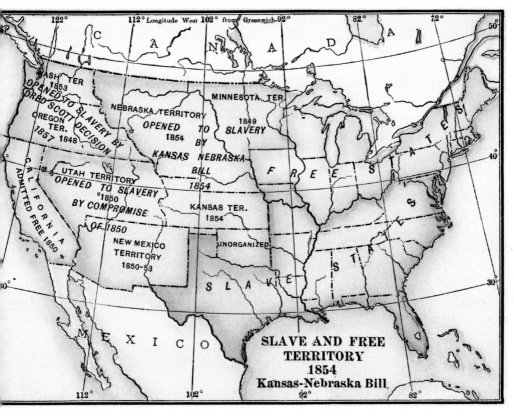

This map shows the free areas and areas allowing slavery as of 1854. The parts labeled "Free States" and "Slave States" reflect the areas that were free and slave at the time of the *Dred Scott* case.

while all territories to the south would allow slavery. As part of the proposal, Missouri—although situated in the "free zone"—would be exempted and enter the Union as a slave state. The northeastern territory of Maine would enter as a free state, thus keeping the number of slave and free states equal. Clay's proposal, known as the Missouri Compromise, was voted upon and accepted by Congress, and Missouri was admitted to the Union as a slave state in 1821.

By 1840, the production of cotton in the southern United States had soared to more than 834 million pounds a year. Cotton had become the most important crop in the world. "King Cotton" ruled the entire southern economy.

With the rapid growth of cotton in the southern United States came the spread of the old plantation system that had originally evolved in the Southeast. By 1845, the cotton industry ranged from the Carolinas in the east to eastern Texas in the west and from Tennessee in the north to Florida in the south. As cotton production expanded into the newly admitted slave states of Missouri and Arkansas, these two areas experienced the most rapid growth in the nation.

Although slavery was still legal in the South, anti-slavery feelings continued to grow nationwide. Those people who were against slavery, called abolitionists, decided to do something to help runaway slaves gain their freedom. They set up a loosely organized system to help runaways escape to free northern states and to Canada. The system was called the "Underground Railroad" because it provided a secret passageway (thus, "underground") for transporting slaves to the North (as if on a "railroad").

When abolitionists working for the "railroad" heard about a runaway slave, they would place the slave under their protection and hide the person until it was safe to move along to another hiding place, or "station," farther north. From the most heavily populated slave states of Alabama, Mississippi, Louisiana, and Arkansas, runaway slaves traveled this "railroad" through Tennessee, Kentucky, Ohio, and Michigan to safety in the northern United States or Canada. At each hiding place, they were given food and shelter until they were ready to move on. The entire trip might take anywhere from several weeks to two or three months. In this way, the abolitionists helped thousands of slaves escape to freedom. Their success angered southern slave owners, who viewed the abolitionists as common thieves out to ruin their way of life.[3]

No doubt Dred Scott had heard about the Underground Railroad, as well as other abolitionist efforts to free slaves. Even in the closed society of the "Deep South," news traveled quickly from one plantation to the next. By the mid-1840s, Scott may have been ready for freedom. Now that his two previous masters, Peter Blow and John Emerson, were dead, his own future was in doubt. Would he remain the property of Mrs. Emerson or be sold to someone else? And, if he remained with the Emerson family, would he be hired out from one job to the next, forced to go wherever he was needed, to work at whatever job had to be done?

Even more important, Scott must have wondered about the fate of his wife and children. It was not unusual in nineteenth-century America for slave families to be broken up and sold to the highest bidders, with husbands, wives, sons, and daughters each going their separate ways, never to meet again. Such were the inhumane horrors of slavery.

In 1843, Scott's worst fears came true when John Emerson's widow lent him and his family to her brother John Sanford. Unfortunately, Sanford was not at all like Emerson. He was a short-tempered, brutal person who constantly abused Dred Scott, his wife, and their children. Finally, unable to withstand any more, Dred Scott asked Mrs. Emerson to set them free. Scott even offered to pay her three hundred dollars for their freedom. But she was not interested. She was perfectly satisfied with Scott and his family working for her brother.

All of this may have been on Scott's mind on April 6, 1846, when he filed a suit for his freedom in the Missouri Circuit Court. Dred Scott's long and difficult quest for freedom had begun.

CHAPTER 3

Suing for Freedom

D red Scott and his wife were fortunate to have moved from the North to Missouri. Unlike other Deep South states, such as Alabama, Mississippi, Florida, and Georgia, Missouri allowed slaves more personal freedoms and rights than most states. Its slave laws were similar to those of Virginia and Kentucky. They provided an opportunity for slaves to file suit with the court for their freedom. Had the Scotts moved almost anywhere else in the South, their ability to pursue their freedom in the courts would most likely not have existed.

Exactly how the suits of Dred and Harriet Scott began and who started them remains a mystery. Some historians believe that Taylor Blow, Scott's longtime friend and childhood companion, may have played a key role. Others feel the suits may have been started by an attorney who felt he could make a large amount of money from the case. As one historian explained, "[The lawyer's] object was to pave the way for a suit against the Emerson estate for the twelve years' wages to which Scott would be entitled should the courts declare that he had been illegally held as a slave since 1834."[1]

There is also the possibility that it was Scott himself who first decided to sue for his freedom. For a slave, he was well-traveled and quite worldly. Although he could neither read nor write and could only make his "mark" on legal documents, many people praised his abilities. A one-time governor of Missouri recalled that "Scott was a very much respected Negro." A St. Louis newspaper reporter, who interviewed Scott after he had gained considerable notoriety from his suits, described him as "illiterate but not ignorant," with a "strong common sense" that had been honed by years of travel with his masters.[2]

Most likely, Scott decided to bring his case to court after years of discussions with other slaves who had done the same, as well as after several talks with old friends, like the Blows, who were sympathetic to his situation.

Both the Blows and their in-laws remained Scott's main supporters throughout the slave's life. One of the reasons for this closeness may have been the resentment the Blow children felt when Scott was sold to Emerson. In particular, Taylor Blow, who was orphaned at the age of twelve, must have felt betrayed. Scott's departure from the Blow family meant the loss of a good friend at a bad time in Taylor's life. Certainly Taylor remained Scott's most loyal supporter throughout the slave's long fight for freedom—and beyond.

In fact, upon Scott's death in 1867, Taylor Blow had his body moved from an abandoned cemetery plot to a more suitable resting place.[3]

Although no historical records prove the fact, it is even possible that the Blows paid for some of Scott's legal fees. Scott himself once stated in an interview that he personally had paid some five hundred dollars in cash and about the same amount in labor. Still, the number of lawyers who eventually worked on the case would undoubtedly have earned far more in fees than one thousand dollars.

A Strong Case

Regardless of who was responsible for what, the Scotts and their attorneys had a strong case under Missouri law. Time and again, the highest court in the state had found that a master who removed a slave to a free state or territory where slavery was banned had thereby set him free.

Unfortunately for the Scotts, Mrs. Emerson and her attorneys were determined to block Scott's attempt to obtain his freedom. Even more unfortunately, the political atmosphere in Missouri was beginning to shift from one that provided a sympathetic climate for the freeing of slaves to one that was much more closed. The Scotts had no way of knowing it at the time, but this shift in climate would ultimately work its way into the state's courts. The Scotts would become casualties of the growing division between the slave and free states in America.

Both Dred and Harriet Scott's cases were virtually identical and are treated as one in this book. When they finally came to court on June 30, 1847, Alexander Hamilton was the presiding, or head, judge. Samuel Mansfield Bay, the former attorney general of Missouri, spoke for the slaves. Mrs. Emerson was represented by George W. Goode, a Virginia lawyer with strong pro-slavery feelings.

On the surface, Scott's attorneys seemed to face a fairly simple task. They needed to prove first that Scott had once lived on free soil and second that he was now held as a slave by Mrs. Emerson, both fairly obvious facts.

In his opening arguments, Scott's new attorney, Samuel M. Bay, called witnesses who had known Dred Scott at Fort Armstrong and Fort Snelling. That established the point of Scott's residence on free soil. For the second point, Bay relied mostly on the testimony, or statements given under oath, of Samuel Russell, who told the court that he had hired the Scotts from Mrs. Emerson, paying money for their use to Mrs. Emerson's father, Alexander Sanford.

Upon cross-examination by Goode, however, Russell admitted that it was actually his wife who had made all the arrangements, and that he knew no more about them than what his wife had told him. That meant that Scott's case had become more difficult to prove, since the jury was told to ignore Russell's testimony. Suddenly, the obvious—that Dred and Harriet Scott were Mrs. Emerson's slaves—turned out to be unprovable. As a result, the jury returned a verdict for the defendant, Mrs. Emerson.

It was a strange twist of fate that, in effect, allowed Mrs. Emerson to keep her slaves because no one had proven that they *were* her slaves.

Requesting a Retrial

Scott's attorneys immediately filed for a new trial, arguing that Russell's testimony had been a surprise to them. Beyond a doubt, Bay insisted, the Scotts could indeed prove that they were slaves.

On December 2, 1847, Judge Hamilton ordered the case to be retried. In response, Mrs. Emerson's lawyer confused the situation further by filing a bill of exceptions to the order for a new trial. The bill was filed because an error had been made in the first trial. If the bill were accepted by the state appellate court, the case would have to be transferred to the Missouri Supreme Court.

In July 1847, the Scotts had obtained a new team of lawyers from the firm of Alexander P. Field and David N. Hall. Field, in particular, was widely known as a tough prosecutor and had a reputation for winning in the courtroom.[4] Mrs. Emerson, on the other hand, kept Goode as her lawyer. In April 1848, the state appellate court heard the appeal. Two months later, it handed down its decision, declaring that, since an order for a retrial had been made by circuit court Judge Hamilton, the Scotts were entitled to obtain a retrial. The decision read in part, "the granting of a new trial cannot be assigned for error."[5] The Scotts were delighted to have won something of a victory, but meanwhile they had lost valuable time in being sent back to the beginning of their search for freedom.

It had become clear that Mrs. Emerson was as determined to keep the Scotts in slavery as the Scotts were to obtain their freedom. Part of the reason may have been that the Blows had become bitter enemies of both the Emersons and the Sanfords, and each family was determined to take whatever steps necessary to win. They got caught up in the process in the spirit of battle that a court trial sometimes sparks—much to Dred and Harriet's disadvantage.

As the day of the retrial drew near, Mrs. Emerson's family hired new attorneys to represent them, Hugh A. Garland and Lyman D. Norris. The case finally reached the circuit court on January 12, 1850, with Judge Hamilton once again presiding. This time, the Scotts clearly established that they had been hired out to several people by Mrs. Emerson, thus proving that they were slaves. The jury found in their favor, and the Scotts were, for the moment, declared free.

Because Mrs. Emerson was unable to get another retrial, she appealed to the Missouri Supreme Court. At this time, the attorneys for both sides signed an agreement recognizing that, since the cases of Dred and Harriet Scott were virtually identical, they would be combined into a single case. The facts of the case were filed in March 1850, but the court did not hear the case until 1852.

Part of the problem the Scotts faced with the delay was that Missouri was beginning to feel increasing political pressure over the question of slavery. The state found itself in an awkward position, bordered on three sides by free territory. Those opposed to slavery were hard at work just outside Missouri's borders, as well as in critical political offices within the state. These forces placed pressure on Missouri's pro-slavery legislature, or law-making body, to guard against anti-slavery laws and uprisings.

A Second Decision

Set against this unstable political background, the state supreme court judges who heard the case decided to reverse the previous court's decision and reject Scott's claim to freedom. Judge William B. Napton was given the task of writing the court's opinion, which he put off for several months. In the meantime, new state lawmakers met, and a statewide election removed both Napton and fellow judge James H. Birch from the state supreme court. This meant that their replacements would have to consider the *Scott* case all over again. It also meant still more time lost—precious time during which those judges who had been leaning toward allowing slaves their freedom were slowly being replaced by more traditional pro-slavery judges.

So in autumn of 1851, Judges William Scott and Hamilton R. Gamble joined Judge John F. Ryland in reconsidering the *Scott* case. The results were predictable. On March 22, 1852, Judge Scott handed down his decision. The court found once again in favor of Mrs. Emerson and ordered the judgment of the lower court to be reversed. In his opinion, Judge Scott wrote,

Every State has the right of determining how far, in a spirit of comity [or recognition of other state's laws], it will respect the laws of other States. Those laws have no intrinsic [or basic] right to be enforced beyond the limits of the State for which they were enacted. The respect allowed them will depend altogether on their conformity to the policy of our [Missouri] institutions. No State is bound to carry into effect enactments conceived in a spirit hostile to that which pervades her own laws.[6]

Judge Scott went on to declare that conflict of state laws was a matter of judgment, something for the court to consider on a case-by-case basis. Then Judge Scott's opinion moved from legal clarification to a political address, taking on the tone of a lecture about the value of slavery as a civilizing institution that had raised the American Negro far above the "miserable" African he had previously been. "We are almost persuaded," he continued, "that the introduction of slavery amongst us was, in the providence of God, who makes the evil passions of men subservient to His own glory, a means of placing that unhappy [black] race within the pale of civilized nations."[7]

Judge Scott's decision was as much political as it was legal. It sounded as if Judge Scott were an angry southern slave owner, not simply an unbiased judge. Nonetheless, the decision stood.

This statue of Dred and Harriet Scott stands in front of the Missouri Supreme Court.

It was a horrible defeat for Dred and Harriet Scott and an amazing victory for Mrs. Emerson. But it was not the end of the Scotts' struggle for freedom. They still had the option of appealing the decision to a higher court.

For reasons still unknown by historians, the Scotts failed to file a prompt appeal with the Supreme Court, which would have been the appropriate next step.

Instead, they waited until Mrs. Emerson remarried, ironically enough to Calvin Chaffee, a staunch opponent of slavery. The Emersons gave the Scotts to Mrs. Emerson's brother, John Sanford. Then, on November 2, 1853, the Scotts filed their case against Sanford in the circuit court of the United States for the District of Missouri. The suit accused Sanford, who was a citizen of New York, of illegally assaulting, holding, and imprisoning Dred Scott, Harriet, and their two daughters, all of whom were citizens of Missouri. On that same day, Taylor Blow insured himself to cover "all the costs and fees which may accrue by reason of the prosecution of the said suit,"[8] and the case was set for the April term in 1854.

On April 7, Sanford and his attorney, Hugh A. Garland, challenged the court's right to hear the case based on the fact that Dred Scott, as a black man descended from slaves of "pure African blood," had therefore never been a true citizen of Missouri. Judge Robert W. Wells, a former Missouri attorney general, denied the challenge, stating that for the purpose of the case, citizenship implied nothing more than residence in a state.

A free Negro, Wells went on to rule, was enough of a citizen to be able to sue in court. Whether or not Scott was free, Wells pointed out, depended upon the laws that applied to Scott's living in free territory. And that could only be determined after a court hearing.

After lengthy legal planning, the case finally came to trial on May 15, 1854. Neither Scott's nor Sanford's lawyers called any new witnesses or introduced any evidence that had not already been presented to the court. The jury then returned a verdict in Sanford's favor. The trial had seemed quick and routine. It was as if everyone involved, from the attorneys and the jurors to Judge Wells himself, saw it as the beginning of a challenge in the US Supreme Court.

As expected, once Judge Wells declined a motion for a new trial, Scott's attorney, Roswell Field, filed a bill of exceptions, the first step necessary to take the case to the highest court in the land.

CHAPTER 4

To the Supreme Court

lmost as soon as Dred Scott's case before the circuit court had begun, it ended. The case itself generated little notoriety. One small mention buried inside the *St. Louis Morning Herald*, the city's main daily newspaper, concluded almost as an afterthought: "Dred [Scott] is, of course, poor and without any powerful friends. But no doubt he will find at the bar of the Supreme Court some able and generous advocate, who will do all he can to establish his right to go free."[1]

An Eloquent Plea

Suddenly the Scotts' work loomed large before them. For starters, they had to find an attorney who could argue the case before the Supreme Court, preferably an experienced lawyer who was willing to donate his fee for legal services. If that failed, they would need to raise the money themselves—not an easy task. Toward that goal, Dred Scott himself dictated the introduction to a twelve-page pamphlet containing a record of the recent trial:

> I have no money to pay anybody at Washington to speak for me. My fellow-men, can any of you help me in my day of trial? Will nobody speak for me at Washington, even without hope of other reward than the blessings of a poor black man and his family? I do not know. I can only pray that some good heart will be moved by pity to do that for me which I cannot do for myself; and that if the right is on my side it may be so declared by the high court to which I have appealed.[2]

It was an eloquent plea, but it fell on deaf ears. Several months passed, and still the Scotts had neither an attorney nor the money necessary to pursue the case. Finally, on Christmas Eve, 1854, in a last-ditch effort, attorney Roswell Field wrote to Montgomery Blair, suggesting that he or some other Washington attorney might serve "the cause of humanity" by taking the Scotts' case. Blair discussed the matter with his family and friends and then agreed to donate his services. He also enlisted the help of *National Era* editor and well-known abolitionist Gamaliel Bailey, who agreed to raise the money necessary for court costs and other related expenses.

Blair Takes the Case

In the Kentucky-born Blair, the Scotts found an extremely able representative. He had been editor of the *Washington Globe*

Montgomery Blair was born into a prominent slave-owning family, but he was a staunch abolitionist. He was a lawyer and he served as Postmaster General in Abraham Lincoln's cabinet.

and served with distinction as a member of President Andrew Jackson's cabinet. He had been part of a movement opposing the Kansas-Nebraska Act, passed earlier in 1854, which canceled the anti-slavery clause of the old Missouri Compromise, opening up a vast new territory to slavery. This delighted most southerners. Blair's wife was the daughter of a former associate justice of the Supreme Court, and Blair himself had argued many cases before the Court.

But Blair would not have an easy time representing Scott. The two attorneys representing Sanford also had excellent legal qualifications. Both Henry S. Geyer, a respected member of the Missouri State Bar, and Reverdy Johnson, a former senator and attorney general under President Zachary Taylor, were among the most respected constitutional lawyers in the country.

So the battle lines were drawn, and the record, or written notes, of *Dred Scott v. Sandford* (the official Court misspelling; the error was never corrected) was delivered to the Supreme Court on December 30, 1854.

While Dred Scott was waiting for the Supreme Court's decision, the effects of the just-passed Kansas-Nebraska Act were beginning to take hold. The Act had divided the unsettled land acquired in the Louisiana Purchase into two vast territories, Kansas and Nebraska.

But both Kansas and Nebraska were north of the line created by the Missouri Compromise, which meant that both territories would have been declared free under the Missouri Compromise. Southern representatives objected.

The last thing they wanted was a shift of political power to the free states of the North. So, Senator Stephen A. Douglas of Illinois developed a plan to solve the problem.

The Kansas-Nebraska Act

Early in 1854, Douglas presented a bill to Congress to help create new states from the Louisiana Territory. To win enough votes to get the bill passed into law, he needed to include conditions that appealed to both northern and southern senators. For the pro-slavery South, Douglas suggested that Congress do away with the Missouri Compromise, with its geographical restrictions on slavery. For the anti-slavery North, he proposed to leave up to the settlers the question of whether new states formed from the Kansas and Nebraska territories would be free or slave.

The Kansas-Nebraska Act reopened many old wounds about slavery. Most northerners were against it. They felt that the Missouri Compromise had adequately addressed the question of slavery in new states, and they wanted to keep the old law. Southerners, on the other hand, liked the new compromise. They realized that Nebraska was too far north ever to become a slave state. But Kansas, with its largely agricultural economy, was a perfect candidate for slavery.

Finally, after several long months of heated debate, the Kansas-Nebraska Act passed Congress, and the Missouri Compromise was cancelled. Before long, northerners who were opposed to slavery began encouraging anti-slavery settlers to move into the territory in an attempt to outvote the settlers who favored slavery. They collected funds, paid European immigrants to move to Kansas, and gave the new settlers farm equipment in exchange for their anti-slavery votes.

Meanwhile, pro-slavery forces from the South were fighting back. On the day of a scheduled election for Kansas' new lawmakers, some five thousand southerners swarmed into the territory from nearby Missouri, took control of the voting booths, and cast four times more ballots than there were registered voters in the territory.

Following the election, the solidly pro-slavery lawmakers met at Shawnee Mission and passed laws favoring slaveholders. These laws limited government officeholders to those who supported slavery. They also provided for the imprisonment of anyone claiming that slavery was either illegal or immoral.

In return, Kansas' anti-slavery forces held an election of their own to choose delegates to the territory's constitutional convention, which would eventually seek the admission of Kansas to the Union as a free state. As a result, by the end of 1855, Kansas had two separate political communities, each with its own governor, lawmakers, and representatives to Congress. Mixed among the two was a "sprinkling of cutthroats attracted by the promise of trouble, while Southerners could count on support from Missouri 'border ruffians' who were always spoiling to 'clean out the abolition crowd.'"[3]

As the two groups poured into Kansas, the pro-slavery forces were greeted by threats and even violence. So much blood was

LIBERTY. THE FAIR MAID OF KANSAS_IN THE HANDS OF THE "BORDER RUFFIANS".

This political cartoon is an attack on the Democratic administration after the passage of the Kansas-Nebraska Act, blaming them for the violence that broke out.

shed during the next few months that the territory was soon given the nickname "Bleeding Kansas."[4]

It was within this explosive political climate that the Supreme Court prepared to hear *Dred Scott v. Sandford*. On February 7, 1856, Blair filed his ten-page brief, or summary of the case, for Dred Scott. Dealing first with the facts of the case, Blair argued that, when Scott had gone to Illinois, the Illinois state constitution specifically forbade slavery in that state. Therefore, Blair argued, as soon as Scott set foot in Illinois, he was free.

But, he asked, was that freedom valid once Scott returned to Missouri? It was, he replied, because of a principle that was valid not only in Missouri, but also in Virginia, Mississippi, and Kentucky, all slave states. It was the principle of permanent emancipation. It meant that, once a slave had been freed, he was free forever. A previous Supreme Court decision was based upon common-law principles that said, "[L]iberty, once admitted, cannot be recalled," and "once free, always free."[5]

Arguing Citizenship

Then Blair turned to a procedural issue, one he thought his opponents would raise in court. Was "a Negro of African descent" a citizen of the United States? Blair admitted that blacks may not have had all the rights of US citizenship, but he insisted that they had at least some. His argument was meant to show that Scott had enough of a right as a citizen to sue in federal court and that Sanford's attorneys could not claim that the Court lacked authority in the case simply because Scott was a slave.

This is where Blair's brief took a curious turn. Only four pages of the ten-page document were devoted to the main task of proving that Scott had a right to be free because he had lived in Illinois, a free state. The rest of the brief concentrated on arguing a point that the lower court had already agreed was valid—that is, that free Negroes were citizens and, thus, qualified to bring suit in a federal court. In short, Blair spent more time and energy defending a point that had already been won than arguing the point that still *needed* to be won before Scott could be declared free: the principle of permanent emancipation.

Arguments Begin

Arguments before the Court, with Chief Justice Roger Brooke Taney presiding, began on February 11, 1856, and continued through Feburary 14. Blair spoke on the first day, followed by his opponents, Geyer and Johnson, on days two and three, with Blair then receiving a response period on the fourth day. Because no witnesses were called before the Court, it was not necessary for Dred Scott to attend the sessions, and he stayed in Missouri.

Unfortunately, no detailed record exists of exactly what each of the attorneys said. The Court in those days did not record oral arguments but instead left the matter up to the lawyers as to whether or not they wished to keep such records. Some newspaper reporters who had heard the arguments reported the highlights, writing that Blair spoke "very ably" on behalf of Dred Scott. His argument, they said, was "a calm, learned and conclusive speech."[6] Most likely, the attorney stressed the same two points he had covered in his brief: that a free Negro has the right to sue as a citizen in federal court; and that a slave once given his freedom in a free state remained free even when he returned to a slave state.

Meanwhile, defense attorney Geyer filed his brief on February 8. Although no copy of the brief is known to exist, he probably made the same points the defense had made in previous cases.

Interestingly enough, few newspapers at the time gave much consideration to the case of Dred Scott, although they carried news of other slave cases, such as the *Sherman Booth* case in Wisconsin, the *Jonathan Lemmon* case in New York, and the *Passmore Williamson* case in Philadelphia. Not even the Washington correspondent for the *St. Louis Daily Missouri Republican* found the *Scott* case important enough to comment on. In fact, the only newspaper to make any mention of substance regarding the case was a Washington paper, which reported, "The public of Washington do not seem to be aware that one of the most important cases ever brought up for adjudication [judgment] by the Supreme Court is now being tried before that august tribunal."[7]

Although no record exists regarding the oral arguments of Sanford's attorneys, Geyer and Johnson, enough was reported in the Washington papers to indicate that they were remarkable in their content.[8] Instead of pursuing the old line of reasoning that Scott was not free because he had lived on a military base or that he had voluntarily returned to the slave state of Missouri or any of the other arguments that had been used in the past, Geyer for the

Roger Brooke Taney served as chief justice from 1836 to 1864. He is best known for his opinion in the *Dred Scott* case.

first time tied the *Dred Scott* case to the constitutionality of the Missouri Compromise. He and Johnson argued that Congress did not have the authority to decide the issue of slavery in the territories. Therefore, the Missouri Compromise was unconstitutional and should be reversed, along with its restrictions against slavery. In effect, Geyer argued, Scott had never been a free man because the Missouri Compromise had been invalid. Until that moment, no one had ever questioned the constitutionality of the Missouri Compromise.[9]

Suddenly, the issue before the Court was no longer whether or not Dred Scott would win his freedom; it was whether or not he had ever been free in the first place. If the Missouri Compromise was invalidated by the Court, there would be no basis for Scott's claim that living in Illinois had made him free. Therefore, when Scott returned to Missouri, he still had the same status he had always had—that of a slave.[10]

Awaiting a Decision

With these arguments completed, the Court considered the case. On the one hand, the arguments behind Scott's case had been clearly and adequately presented. On the other, Sanford's arguments were equally strong, although the attorneys for Sanford took an entirely new approach to their presentation. Instead of concentrating on the arguments that concerned Scott, the attorneys for Sanford broke new ground.[11]

Speculation about the Court's ruling raged even before the justices met to consult on the case. If the participants had seemed confused about the differing approaches used by the attorneys, the newspaper reports of the trial were even more confusing. One paper suggested that the Court would be deciding two issues: Congress' authority to control slavery in the territories, and the right of slaveholders to take their slaves into free states without surrendering ownership.[12] Another paper suggested the Court would examine Scott's quest for freedom in light of his voluntary return to Missouri and slavery.[13] Still another insisted that the Court would overlook the question of the constitutionality of the Missouri Compromise and concentrate instead on the right of blacks to be citizens of the United States.[14]

The confusion surrounding what had taken place in the courtroom and how the Court would vote was reflected in a larger sense by the confusion in Congress over the entire slavery issue. In passing both the Missouri Compromise and the Kansas-Nebraska Act, Congress had decided that disputes over slavery and personal freedom should be appealed directly to the Supreme Court, thus avoiding the legalities of slavery. Surprisingly, not until Geyer's attack in his oral arguments had the matter come before the Court. Although *Dred Scott* had begun as a relatively simple question of one man's freedom, it had suddenly grown to be a much more complex issue encompassing Congress's right to regulate slavery. As Professor David M. Potter put it, the Court "would decide to rush in where Congress had feared to tread."[15]

On February 22, the Court met to discuss *Dred Scott*, but the meeting was short, and no conclusions were reached. The Court met again a few days later to consider the case and again failed to reach any conclusions. The justices consulted yet again on April 7, 9, and 12 and still could not reach a decision. Finally, they decided to reargue the case in the hopes of "clarifying the law and making a final judgment possible."[16] On May 12, the Court ordered the case to be reargued in the fall.

By then, many people had begun to question what they perceived to be the Court's political motivation. Some politicians felt the southern Democrats on the Court had deliberately postponed judgment until after the 1856 presidential election so as not to tip the balance in favor of the Republicans. Even Abraham Lincoln shared the view that southern pro-slavery Democrats were attempting to sway the Court in the hopes of seeing the Missouri Compromise overturned. This, he felt, would pave the way for the legalization of slavery throughout the country.[17]

James E. Harvey, a reporter for the *New York Tribune*, suggested that the Court had decided to postpone its decision in order to prevent Justice John McLean, a strong supporter of the Missouri Compromise, from delivering a passionate dissent that might launch him into the political arena as the Republican nominee for president of the United States. This argument loses some of its strength, however, from the realization that McLean had voted along with the other justices for reargument.

While some of the justices may have been politically influenced, most simply needed more information before they could reach an informed decision. It would be seven more months before the case would come before the Court again.

CHAPTER 5

To Court Again

I
n the seven months before *Dred Scott v. Sandford* came up for reargument before the US Supreme Court, the split between the North and the South over the subject of slavery had exploded. On May 21, 1856, a mob of pro-slavery "border ruffians" rode into Lawrence, Kansas, the center of anti-slavery Kansas Territory, and nearly destroyed the city. The following day, Preston S. Brooks, South Carolina's pro-slavery representative, physically assaulted Charles Sumner, a senator from the anti-slavery state of Massachusetts in the US senate chambers, seriously injuring him. The assault came in response to Sumner's earlier vocal attacks on slavery.

Two days later, on May 24, John Brown launched a raid at Pottawatomie Creek, Kansas, killing five pro-slavery

Abolitionist John Brown executed five pro-slavery supporters in retaliation for the sacking of Lawrence, Kansas, and the beating of Senator Charles Sumner.

supporters. It was the first of a long series of violent acts by Brown, who believed that southern slaves could be freed only by force.

As the gap between the North and the South continued to grow, the Republicans and Democrats began their campaigns for the presidency. The Republicans nominated John C. Fremont and William L. Dayton as their presidential and vice-presidential candidates. Their strong anti-slavery platform declared that "the Constitution confers upon Congress sovereign power over the Territories of the United States" and that Congress had "both the right and the duty" to prohibit slavery in the territories.[1]

The Democrats nominated James Buchanan and John C. Breckinridge under a platform that stressed "popular sovereignty," which called for the question of slavery in the territories to be decided by the residents of those territories. The presidential election of November 4, 1856, resulted in a slim victory for the Democrats and a continuing debate over slavery in Congress.

It was in this politically charged climate that, on December 2, 1856, Henry S. Geyer filed his brief for defendant John A. Sanford. In response to an order from the Court, Geyer spent a great deal of time talking about the question of citizenship. To be a citizen eligible to sue in the federal courts, according to Geyer, a person had first to be a citizen of the state in which he lived. Missouri did not grant citizenship to blacks—not even free blacks; therefore, Dred Scott was not a citizen.

THE GREAT AMERICAN BUCK HUNT OF 1856.

This political cartoon by N. Currier favors the political candidate Millard Fillmore of the American Party, as he and Fremont take aim at a "buck" (James Buchanan) that makes a run for the White House.

Geyer also addressed the difference between permanent and temporary residence. Scott's residence in Illinois was only temporary, he stressed, adding that a slave traveling with his owner in or through a free state is not automatically granted freedom.

On December 15, Montgomery Blair filed an additional brief to support the one he had filed earlier on behalf of plaintiff Dred Scott. In it, Blair countered Geyer's argument about permanent versus temporary residence. He wrote at length about the constitutionality of the Missouri Compromise. He argued that Congress had had absolute power over US territories since the 1780s. This power, he said, included the right to limit slavery. Because Congress had such power, he concluded, the constitutionality of the Missouri Compromise was not in question.

With both briefs having been submitted, the oral arguments for *Dred Scott v. Sandford* were scheduled. All nine justices were present on December 15, 1856, when Blair, joined by Boston attorney George Ticknor Curtis to help argue the question of the power of Congress over slavery in the territories, opened the arguments for Scott. Taking the entire three hours allotted to the case the first day, Blair devoted considerable time to the fact that Dred Scott was a citizen and a proper plaintiff, thus hoping to satisfy the Court's questions concerning authority.

Next, Blair argued the primary merits, or facts of the case. He pointed out first that the states had the absolute right to prohibit slavery and, second, that Congress had the absolute right to make decisions affecting slavery within the territories. Even such well-known southerners as John C. Calhoun, he said, had accepted the power of Congress to prohibit slavery in the territories. Thus, he said, when Dred Scott came to live in Illinois, he had to be free, because slavery in Illinois had been banned.

On the following day, Geyer argued the case for Sanford. Like Blair the day before, he used all three hours allotted to him. He stressed the main point he had made in his brief, that Scott, as a Negro, could not be a citizen of the United States and therefore could not sue in federal court.

Geyer then turned his attention to the facts of the case,

arguing that Scott's temporary residence in Illinois did not qualify him for freedom. The Illinois state constitution, he said, simply prevented the state from establishing slavery, but it had no effect on a slave brought into the state, especially if that slave was only passing through the state or living there temporarily. He insisted this was the case with Dred Scott. He then argued that the Missouri Compromise was a violation of the authority of the people of the United States, because it denied them power over local governments, power that he said the Constitution of the United States had guaranteed them. The Missouri Compromise was therefore unconstitutional and thus null and void. He concluded the second day's remarks by insisting that Scott could not claim freedom simply because he lived in Illinois.

The following day, Reverdy Johnson, also appearing on Sanford's behalf, argued that the Constitution of the United States allowed for the right of citizens to own property, but that it did not consider Negroes to be citizens. Congress, he pointed out, could do nothing that was harmful to any one state. Yet, by prohibiting slavery in the territories, Congress was enacting laws harmful to the interests of the slave states. That was reason enough, he concluded, to find the Missouri Compromise to be unconstitutional.

On the fourth day of oral arguments, all four attorneys addressed the Court. Although each supported his previous arguments, Curtis also presented a lengthy discussion of the constitutionality of the Missouri Compromise in Scott's favor. He pointed out that, under Article IV, Section 3, of the

Constitution, Congress had the power to "dispose of and make all needful Rules and Regulations respecting the Territory or other Property belonging to the United States." This, Curtis concluded, was proof that the writers of the Constitution had intended from the start that Congress should have absolute power over a territory as long as it remained a territory. Not until a territory became a state could that state alone have the right to decide upon its institutions, including slavery. Therefore, he concluded, the Missouri Compromise was constitutional, and Dred Scott was entitled to his freedom because he had lived in free Illinois. Curtis's arguments for Scott were both well-presented and sound, and Blair must have been grateful at having received such solid last-minute help from so talented a constitutional lawyer.

Four Questions

At the conclusion of the reargument, the case was out of all four attorneys' hands and under the consideration of the Court, which was now faced with answering four questions placed before it. Two of the questions were procedural, and two of them concerned the case's merits, or points of fact.

1. *Was there a plea in abatement before the Court?*
   A plea in abatement is a request to dismiss a case because it lacks merit. If so, then the Court would refuse to rule on the case. Scott's counsel hoped the Court would decide that there was no plea in abatement.

2. *Was Dred Scott a citizen of Missouri and thus able to bring a suit in a federal court?*

In answering this question, precedent was on Scott's side, because the previous lower court decision had declared that a free Negro was a citizen under the diverse-citizenship clause. If the Court decided against Scott on this question, the case would be decided in Sanford's favor. If the Court decided with Scott, the justices would go on to continue the case on its merits.

3 *Was Scott a free man because he had lived in Illinois Territory?*

The answer to this question depended on whether the Court found Scott's residence at Fort Armstrong to be permanent or merely temporary. If the Court decided in Scott's favor, he would win the case. If it did not, the justices would need to answer the last question.

4. *Was Scott a free man because he had lived at Fort Snelling in Minnesota, a free territory as outlined by the Missouri Compromise?*

An answer to this question would require a ruling on the constitutionality of the Missouri Compromise's restriction on slavery.

Given the strong pro-slavery makeup of the Court, it seemed likely that its decision would go against Scott. But the Court was concerned with more than making decisions. It was also concerned with the way it reached its decision, something that could have strong political overtones in a nation deeply divided on the question of slavery.

It could avoid a decision entirely, of course, by simply answering the first question positively and the second negatively. The case would be dismissed for lack of jurisdiction, which is the power, right, and authority to interpret and apply the law. That would undoubtedly anger many people opposed to slavery and leave the slavery question up in the air. But the justices were so strongly divided on the question of the plea in abatement that it seemed unlikely that they would take this course.

Another solution would be to uphold the decision of the lower Missouri court, relying on another case, *Strader v. Graham*, as a legal precedent. The *Strader* case had involved a group of slaves whose Kentucky owner allowed them to work briefly in Ohio. The Supreme Court had found that the rights of the slaves were based on the laws of the state from which they had come (Kentucky), rather than on the laws of Ohio. Once the slaves had returned to Kentucky, they again became the property of their owner. By using the *Strader* principle as the basis for returning negative answers to both questions three and four, the Court would uphold the decision of the lower court, and Scott would lose his bid for freedom.

How would the Court rule? An anxious nation was eager to learn.

CHAPTER 6

The Court's Decision

C hristmas—always a cheerful, heart-warming time of year for Dred Scott and his family—came late in 1856. That is, December 25 arrived right on time, of course, but missing were those cheery warm feelings that once accompanied the holiday's arrival.

That year, Christmas for the Scott family was a time of mixed feelings. Throughout the course of the Supreme Court hearing, Dred and Harriet had worked as laborers under the supervision of the Court, which allowed them to be hired out to perform various odd jobs in and around their Missouri home. The money they earned was deposited in a bank account and would be released following the Court's decision. If the decision went in favor of John Sanford, he would receive the money. If, on the other hand, it went in favor of the Scotts, they would receive all the proceeds.

The Scotts had never dreamed that the Court's proceedings would take so long or become so involved. Scott himself later told a local newspaper interviewer that he did not understand what all "the fuss" was about. But fuss there was. In fact, by the time the New Year had dawned, the "great case," which several newspapers had come to call it, had caused heated debate from the local barber shop to the floor of Congress. Everywhere people were talking about *Dred Scott v. Sandford*, not because of their interest in the outcome of Scott's bid for freedom so much as from their desire to see how the Court would decide on the question of slavery.

Unexpected Delays

But the Court's decision was unexpectedly delayed when, on January 3, 1857, Justice Peter Daniel's wife died in a fiery accident. The grief-stricken Daniels was unable to attend another session until mid-February, and it was then that the Court held its first conference on *Dred Scott*.

At that conference, two notable things happened. First, Justice Samuel Nelson decided to join four other justices who believed that the plea in abatement was not a consideration of the Court and therefore would not play a role in the Court's decision. This created a majority opinion and was good news for Scott.

Second, the Court's five southern justices favored doing away with the slavery restriction of the Missouri

Judge Samuel Nelson served on the Supreme Court from 1845 to 1872. He was the only successful appointment made by President John Tyler.

Compromise. Justices John McLean and Benjamin Curtis favored keeping the Compromise intact, while Samuel Nelson and Robert Grier favored maintaining the circuit court's decision, thus in effect avoiding entirely a decision on whether or not the Compromise was constitutional. In time, the five southern justices decided to join with Nelson and Grier in upholding the lower court's decision, and Nelson was appointed to write the opinion of the Court. No decision on the citizenship issue or on the power of Congress to regulate slavery in the territories would be made—this was more good news for Scott.

But as time passed, the justices became aware that the public had come to expect a decision on the question of the constitutionality of the Missouri Compromise. What had begun as a simple question of ownership had grown into something far more complex. Plus, political pressure from the justices' peers and associates, especially those of the southern justices, was beginning to take its toll. Several members of the Court expressed concerns about the need to save the South from the disgrace and humiliation to which northerners opposed to slavery had been subjecting them. Justice Alexander H. Stephens went so far as to inform his brother that he was urging the court to a prompt decision, expecting that it would settle the Missouri Compromise issue in the South's favor once and for all.

Even President-elect James Buchanan entered the dispute when he wrote his close friend Justice John Catron on February 3, requesting information on the likelihood of the Court's findings. He wanted to know the outcome, he said, so that he could mention the issue in his inaugural address on March 4, 1857. In fact, Buchanan was hoping that the Court would rule on the constitutionality of the Missouri Compromise so that he could support its findings. Catron's reply of February 10 was disappointing. In his letter, he revealed that the case would be decided as early as Saturday, February 14, and that the Court would probably not make a decision regarding whether Congress had power over slavery in the territories.

An Opinion, Take One

But Nelson did not begin work on his opinion until the weekend of February 14–15, when he wrote a short opinion of about five thousand words. In it, Nelson wrote that the Court would not rule on the plea in abatement. About Scott having lived in Illinois, Nelson wrote that his status as a slave or a free man depended entirely upon where he resided at the time the question was being answered. "The laws of each [state]," he added, "have no extraterritorial operation within the jurisdiction of another [state], except such as may be voluntarily conceded by her laws or courts of justice."[1] If Scott had become free while in Illinois, Nelson reasoned, he did so because Illinois refused to recognize and enforce the slave laws of Missouri. Once he returned to Missouri, however, Scott returned to that state's laws and to slavery. "Has the law of Illinois any greater force within the jurisdiction of Missouri than the laws of the latter [state] within the former? Certainly not. They stand upon equal footing."[2]

In short, Nelson was saying that the laws of one state were no more or less binding on a person than those of another.

Then Nelson wrote that, once Scott returned from Minnesota to Missouri, the slave state's laws took effect, and Scott was bound by them. Therefore, Scott was still a slave.

An Opinion, Take Two

No sooner had Nelson finished writing his opinion than the Court changed its mind and decided to tackle the much touchier issue of the constitutionality of the Missouri Compromise. The threat of Justices McLean and Curtis to write extensive and dissenting opinions disagreeing with all aspects of the case—including the constitutional issue— had forced the Court to reconsider its ruling on the Missouri Compromise. Justice James M. Wayne then moved that Chief Justice Roger Taney write the Court's new opinion.

So on March 6, 1857, Taney began reading a summary of his opinion in a crowded courtroom: Slaves were not US citizens and could not sue in federal courts. Also, the Missouri Compromise was unconstitutional, and Congress did not have the authority to prohibit slavery in the territories. Following that, Nelson and Catron read their relatively short opinions. The next day, McLean and Curtis read theirs for nearly five hours. But the press had heard little more than the incendiary remarks of the chief justice. Taney's decision was lavishly praised by southern pro-slavery Democrats and furiously condemned by northern anti-slavery Republicans.

When Taney's full opinion had still not been released for publication on May 13, Curtis wrote the chief justice and demanded an explanation, declaring his right to examine the Court's official opinion. It was an opinion that Taney was rumored to be revising after hearing other opinions. Tensions between Curtis and Taney grew as the two sent angry letters back and forth.[3]

Taney's Official Opinion

Finally, in late May, Taney's official opinion was released, and Curtis was able to compare it to what he remembered of Taney's oral version. He had heard it twice before, once in conference and then again in Court on March 6. Curtis concluded that "upwards of eighteen pages," or nearly a third of Taney's opinion, had been revised or added. "No one can read them," Curtis said, "without perceiving that they are in reply to my opinion."[4]

Curtis insisted that Taney was wrong in changing his opinion at so late a date, while Taney replied that he had done no such thing. The heated disagreement eventually drove the two justices so far apart that Curtis submitted his resignation from the Court the following September. Publicly, Curtis named the low salary of associate justices as a reason for resigning. In private, however, he admitted to friends that he could not "again feel confidence in the Court and that willingness to cooperate with them which is essential to the satisfactory discharge of my duties."[5]

So the case of Dred Scott had finally come to an end. The Supreme Court had decided once and for all that Dred Scott was still a slave and that the Missouri Compromise was unconstitutional. Congress had never had the authority to use slavery or anti-slavery status as a "measuring stick" for admitting new states into the Union. The long-awaited ruling was not well received.

CHAPTER 7

After *Dred Scott*

N ews of the decision in *Dred Scott v. Sandford* spread like a prairie fire across the land. From the papers to the pulpit, from the people to the politicians, everyone had an opinion about the Court's decision. It seemed as if no one remained unaffected—or unmoved.

Members of the American Party and Free-Soilers who opposed slavery only the day before the verdict was read had been working for the release of all slaves. Suddenly, they were forced to redirect their anger toward the Taney Court. They were determined to see *Dred Scott* reversed in order to stop the spread of slavery throughout the country. And the best way to do that, they realized, was by pressuring Congress to pass new laws.[1]

By gaining control of the executive and legislative branches of government, the Republicans believed they could place pressure on the Court to reconsider its decision.[2] Better still, with Chief Roger Taney now eighty years old and several other justices not much younger, it was clear that several members

C. C. Chaffee.

Mass.

31

of the Court would soon be leaving. Those opposed to slavery wanted a Republican in the White House to nominate anti-slavery replacements on the Court.[3]

A Lot of Explaining to Do

Meanwhile, only days after the Court's decision, the *Argus* of Springfield, Massachusetts, printed an article stating that Dred Scott was not actually the property of Alexander Sanford but, rather, of Dr. Calvin Clifford Chaffee, the anti-slavery Republican congressman who had recently married Irene Emerson. In the article, the paper suggested that Chaffee had some serious explaining to do about his relationship to Scott and the most famous Supreme Court case in the land.

In a reply appearing in the *Springfield Daily Republican* on March 16, 1857, Chaffee wrote that

the defendant [Sanford] was and is the only person who had or has any power in the matter, and neither myself nor any member of my family were consulted in relation to, or even knew of the existence of the suit till after it was noticed for trial, when we learned it in an accidental way.[4]

When Mrs. Chaffee (formerly Emerson) moved with Dr. Chaffee from St. Louis, she had simply left Scott and his

---

Dr. Calvin Clifford Chaffee was called a hypocrite due to his involvement with the Emerson family, which was at odds with his stance as an abolitionist.

family in the care of her father. It was not until February 1857 that she informed her husband that Dred Scott, the plaintiff in the Supreme Court suit, was actually the slave of her deceased husband. "Possessed of no power to control, refused all right to influence the course of the defendant in the case," Chaffee wrote, he could do nothing to affect the case and was in fact advised by his own attorney to remain quiet until the case had been decided by the Supreme Court.[5]

Path to Freedom

Now that the Court had given its decision, Chaffee took immediate steps to pave the way for Scott's freedom. On May 26, 1857, he executed a quitclaim deed in which he, his wife, and his stepdaughter gave up all rights and interests they may have had in Dred Scott and his family, transferring all rights to Taylor Blow, Scott's longtime friend. Once that was done, Dred and Harriet Scott appeared with Blow in the Missouri Circuit Court, before Judge Alexander Hamilton, and acknowledged the papers granting their freedom. After eleven years of intense legal battles, Dred Scott, his wife, and their daughters were finally free.

Strangely enough, John Sanford never witnessed Scott's freedom. By the time the Supreme Court had rendered its decision, Sanford had been institutionalized for insanity. He died in an asylum in New York on May 5, 1857. Scott himself, after less than two years of freedom and several weeks of illness, died in St. Louis on Friday, September 17, 1858, and

The inscription on Dred Scott's grave says he was "freed from slavery by his friend Taylor Blow."

was buried in an unmarked grave in Wesleyan Cemetery. Nine years later, Taylor Blow had Scott reburied in the family plot at Calvary Cemetery in northern St. Louis.

Upon Scott's death in 1858, newspapers around the country carried stories of the most famous slave in the nation. Some Republican anti-slavery papers recounted the story of the long and grueling trial that was still tearing the nation apart.

Harpers Ferry

One year later, in October 1859, anti-slavery activist John Brown, who had murdered five pro-slavery men during the fighting at Pottawatomie Creek, Kansas, gathered three of his sons and fifteen other followers, both white and black, and staged a daring raid on the federal arsenal at Harpers Ferry, Virginia. Brown succeeded in capturing the arsenal, but his uprising was doomed to failure. The ragtag band of poorly armed men was no match for a detachment of US Marines under the leadership of Colonel Robert E. Lee and Lieutenant J. E. B. ("Jeb") Stuart.[6]

After a bloody standoff during which the arsenal was subjected to a withering barrage of fire, Brown and eight men who had survived the assault were captured, tried, and convicted. Brown himself was hanged shortly thereafter. Before he died, he wrote a warning to a nation in turmoil: "I, John Brown, am now quite certain that the crimes of this guilty land will never be purged away but with blood. I had, as I now think, vainly flattered myself that without much bloodshed it might be done."[7]

The raid at Harpers Ferry, led by John Brown, was unsuccessful, but it showed that feelings for and against slavery were running high.

Debate on Slavery

Meanwhile, during autumn of the previous year, two political candidates from Illinois, a Democrat and a Republican, had agreed to argue the slavery issue in a series of political debates. The Democrat was Stephen A. Douglas, the sponsor of the Kansas-Nebraska Act and a senator running for reelection in Illinois. Douglas was an able leader who hoped someday to become president of the United States.

The anti-slavery Republican challenger for the Senate was Abraham Lincoln, a lawyer from Springfield, Illinois. Unlike Douglas, Lincoln was unknown outside Illinois. But his friends and neighbors admired his honesty, humor, and ability to win legal cases.[8]

Lincoln had spent a great deal of time thinking about the political issues of the day, especially the issue of slavery. In accepting the Republican nomination for the Senate, he had said:

"A house divided against itself cannot stand." I believe this government cannot endure, permanently, half slave and half free. I do not expect the Union to be dissolved; I do not expect the house to fall; but I do expect it will cease to be divided. It will become all one thing, or all the other. Either the opponents of slavery will arrest the further spread of it, and place it where the public mind shall rest in the belief that it is in the course of ultimate extinction; or its advocates will push it forward, till it shall become alike lawful in all the States, old as well as new, North as well as South.[9]

Those southerners who heard Lincoln speak were sure that he intended to end slavery in the South. They began to fear for their economic livelihood and way of life.[10]

In their debate at Freeport, Illinois, Lincoln and Douglas launched arguments that were as different as their political backgrounds. "Should slavery be permitted in the territories?"

someone asked. Let the settlers in the territories decide for themselves, said Douglas, arguing for states' rights. Lincoln, on the other hand, supported the rights of the federal government. He suggested slavery could be lawful in the South, but *only* in the South. He wanted slavery kept out of the territories and the newly forming states.[11]

Although neither candidate was a clear winner in the debate, Douglas went on to win the race for the Senate. Lincoln, on the other hand, won many new friends and loyal supporters for his outspoken views against slavery.

An Important Election

Two years later, Lincoln was nominated as the Republican party's presidential candidate. In every state, people came to listen to what this thoughtful man had to say about the events and issues of the day.

Running for the Democrats was none other than Stephen A. Douglas. But Douglas was having difficulty attracting both northern and southern voters. Voters in the North were leery of him because of his slavery stance in the Lincoln-Douglas debates. After all, Douglas had never come out against slavery, and that bothered many northerners.[12]

In the South, voters distrusted Douglas because he had not clearly stated that slavery should be made legal. Instead, he seemed to straddle the fence by insisting that the settlers of each territory and new state should decide for themselves whether or not they wanted slavery. Many southerners were still deeply committed to the institution of slavery and simply could not support such a candidate.

As southern Democrats by the thousands turned away from both Lincoln and Douglas, a third man emerged as a political candidate for the presidency. He was John C. Breckinridge of Kentucky. Breckinridge ran on a platform that supported the right to include slavery in all existing territories as well as in all new states.

By the time of the election, southerners split their votes between Douglas and Breckinridge. Meanwhile, Lincoln had won a great majority of the votes in the North, and with them, the presidency of the United States. For the first time in US history, the nation had elected a president who clearly represented the goals and beliefs of only one section of the country, the anti-slavery North.

Abraham Lincoln was aware of the problems that his victory had created. He understood that the division between North and South was likely to grow worse before it got better. But he was determined to save the Union at any cost. The United States, he believed, had to remain united.[13]

The South Secedes

On December 20, 1860, on the streets of Charleston, South Carolina, bells rang out, and cheering and singing filled the air. It was as though a huge circus had come to town.

But it was no circus. It was news that South Carolina had just voted to withdraw from the Union, barely one month after Lincoln's election as president. The *Charleston Mercury* newspaper carried the story:

Passed at 1:15 o'clock p.m., December 20, 1860, an ordinance to dissolve the Union between the state of South Carolina, and other states united with her under the compact entitled the Constitution of the United States of America.

A sectional party [the Republican Party] has elected a man [Abraham Lincoln] to the high office of President of the United States whose opinions and purposes are hostile to slavery. He is to be entrusted with the administration of the common government because he has declared that that government cannot endure permanently half slave, half free. On the fourth of March next this party will take possession of the government. The guarantees of the Constitution will then no longer exist and the equal rights of the states will be lost. The slaveholding states will then no longer have the power of self-government or self-protection, and the federal government will have become their enemy.[14]

Before long, Mississippi, Florida, Alabama, Georgia, Louisiana, and Texas, the states of the Deep South, joined South Carolina in seceding from, or leaving, the Union. On February 4, 1861, representatives of these states met in Montgomery, Alabama, and drew up a constitution for a new nation, to be called the Confederate States of America. These states modeled their constitution after that of the United States, with one major difference. It stated flatly that no laws could be passed that denied the right to own Negro slaves. Jefferson Davis, who had once fought alongside Lincoln in the Black Hawk War, was elected president of the Confederacy.

As the date for Abraham Lincoln's inauguration drew closer, people wondered how Lincoln would react to the Southern States leaving the Union. Finally, on March 4, 1861, an anxious crowd gathered in Washington, DC, to hear Lincoln's inaugural address. The new president took his oath of office and began his speech. After the first few words, the audience knew exactly where Lincoln stood: Under the Constitution of the United States, Lincoln said, a permanent Union of the states had been created. None of these states could lawfully leave the Union. It was up to the president to see that the laws of the nation were carried out in all states.

Toward the end of his speech, Lincoln's words turned hopeful as he appealed to the South to return to the Union:

In *your* hands, my dissatisfied fellow countrymen, and not in mine, is the momentous issue of civil war. The government will not assail you. You can have no conflict without yourselves the aggressors. You have no oath registered in heaven to destroy the government, while I shall have the most solemn one to "preserve, protect, and defend" it. ... I am loath to close. We are not enemies but friends. We must not be enemies. Though passion may have strained, it must not break our bonds of affection.[15]

The words had little effect on the South. In the early morning hours of April 12, 1861, a Confederate force led by General Pierre G. T. Beauregard opened fire on Fort Sumter, a United States military post in Charleston Harbor, South Carolina. The Civil War had begun.

CHAPTER 8

Abraham Lincoln Acts

A s if Abraham Lincoln hadn't enough on his mind with the opening of the Civil War, Chief Justice Taney continued to taunt him. By that time emaciated and nearing the end of his life, Taney was nonetheless resentful over popular reaction to his *Dred Scott* decision. He was convinced that the decision had been right. He was just as convinced that Lincoln had gone far beyond the powers of the presidency and that the president's actions needed to be sharply curtailed.[1]

For three years, Taney opposed nearly every action taken by Lincoln in the name of the federal government. When Lincoln suspended writs of habeas corpus, which provides a prisoner with the right to a prompt appearance in court, in an effort to stop the activities of anti-war demonstrators and Confederate

Abraham Lincoln was photographed on August 9, 1863, by Alexander Gardner. Lincoln was in office from 1861 to April 15, 1865, the date of his assassination.

sympathizers, Taney objected. He strongly believed that no one could be arrested and imprisoned without a speedy trial, not even during time of war.

When Confederate supporter John Merryman was arrested and brought to Fort McHenry in Baltimore, Taney issued a writ of habeas corpus and ordered General George Cadwalader, the military commander at Fort McHenry, to bring Merryman to the federal court for trial. Cadwalader refused Taney's order because he recognized Lincoln's authority to suspend the right of habeas corpus.[2]

Taney then sent a US marshal to arrest the general for contempt of court. But when the marshal arrived, he was sternly turned away by a military guard. In response, an angry Taney wrote an opinion, *Ex Parte Merryman*, in which he declared that only Congress, and not the president, had the power to suspend the right of habeas corpus.[3] Taney sent a copy of his opinion to Lincoln, and Lincoln shared it with his attorney general, who advised the president that Taney was wrong. This angered Taney all the more.[4] Not long after, when the Supreme Court decided in a 5-4 decision that Lincoln had the power to blockade the southern coast, Taney disagreed. When Lincoln signed the Conscription Act authorizing the drafting of men for war service, Taney complained that it was unconstitutional. The chief justice even went so far as to rule against Lincoln's Emancipation Proclamation, which freed the slaves in the Confederacy.

Finally, in 1864, the ongoing war between the cantankerous Taney and the president of the United States came to an end when Chief Justice Taney died at age eighty-seven. At a memorial service held by members of the Boston Bar Association, a generous tribute to Taney's long and varied career was delivered by none other than Benjamin R. Curtis, the former justice who had clashed so often and violently with Taney during the *Dred Scott* case.

In 1868, three years after the Civil War ended in a victory for the Union, Congress passed the Fourteenth Amendment to the Constitution. It declared that Negroes, as well as all other people born or naturalized in the United States, were citizens and entitled to all citizenship benefits equally. In an ironic twist of fate, it took four years of bloody battle, a presidential proclamation declaring the freedom of enslaved blacks, and a constitutional amendment to overturn the damage that Chief Justice Taney and the Supreme Court had done in only a few fateful weeks.

But the freeing of America's slaves and the guarantee of their equal rights of citizenship under the law were not the end of *Dred Scott*. The decision was condemned and criticized by legal historians as a "ghastly error" and a "ruinous decision."[5] Nonetheless, it has served as a legal precedent for hundreds of cases ever since, from Reconstruction to civil rights.

In the end, it was neither the decision of the Supreme Court nor the opinion of Roger Taney that marked the very first step toward the freeing of America's enslaved blacks. It was not the Civil War or a constitutional amendment. It was not even the famed Emancipation Proclamation. It was the determination of a highly respected man with a strong streak of common sense and a willingness to fight for what he felt was right. It was the desire of one man to be free, a yearning for all men everywhere to be free, and that one man's willingness to risk everything in his innate desire to help make that freedom happen. It was a man named Dred Scott.

CHAPTER 9
The Reconstruction Years

When the *Dred Scott* decision came down from the Court, it created instant nationwide reaction. Throughout history, the case has been regarded by legal and constitutional scholars as one of the worst US Supreme Court decisions in the history of the Court. Still, no one can doubt that it played an important role in American history.

If it hadn't been for the deep resentment and bitter reaction to the Court's decision, the question of the legality of owning slaves in America might have gone unchallenged for decades.

Instead, the long and costly Civil War and the constitutional amendments banning slavery once and for all set a deeply divided nation on the right course. If nothing else, the disastrous ruling by Chief Justice Taney in *Dred Scott v. Sandford* emboldened America's legislature—both the House of Representatives and the US Senate—to look more closely into its citizens' rights and what it might do to protect them.

The Reconstruction Amendments

Following the end of the Civil War, Congress quickly enacted the Thirteenth, Fourteenth, and Fifteenth Amendments to the US Constitution, which came to be known as the Reconstruction amendments.

- The **Thirteenth Amendment** (1865) outlawed slavery. It says in Section 1: "Neither slavery nor involuntary servitude, except as a punishment for crime whereof the party shall have been duly convicted, shall exist within the United States, or any place subject to their jurisdiction."

- The **Fourteenth Amendment** (1868) gave US citizenship to blacks by requiring the states to consider the life, liberty, and property of *all* persons to be equal under law. Section 1 says:

  > All persons born or naturalized in the United States, and subject to the jurisdiction thereof, are citizens of the United States and of the State wherein they reside. No State shall make or enforce any law which shall abridge the privileges or immunities of citizens of the United States; nor shall any State deprive

any person of life, liberty, or property, without due process of law; nor deny to any person within its jurisdiction the equal protection of the laws.

- The **Fifteenth Amendment** (1870) prohibits racial discrimination in voting rights. Section 1 says: "The right of citizens of the United States to vote shall not be denied or abridged by the United States or by any State on account of race, color, or previous condition of servitude."

Each of the three Reconstruction amendments contains a clause granting Congress the power to enforce the law. Congress was quick to use its newfound powers, soon passing a series of civil rights' statutes whose goals were to protect recently freed slaves from discrimination based on their race.

By the latter part of the nineteenth century, the US Supreme Court was forced to confront a number of issues relating to the interpretation of the Reconstruction amendments. The wording of the amendments and how that wording should be interpreted was not always clear. In an era when an individual state's rights were considered superior to the rights of the federal government, the Court often approached the entire concept of civil rights gingerly so as not to upset the states or risk usurping their powers.[1]

In *United States v. Cruikshank* (1875),[2] the Court went so far as to dismiss charges against an armed mob of whites

Blacks are shown gathering their dead after the massacre in Colfax, Louisiana.

who had surrounded a courthouse in which a large group of blacks were holding a public assembly in Colfax, Louisiana. The whites set fire to the building, killing nearly a hundred people in the process.

The ringleaders were put on trial and convicted by a lower court of murder under the Force Act, passed by Congress in 1870, which made conspiring "to injure, oppress, threaten, or intimidate any person in the free exercise of any right or privilege secured to him by the

Constitution or laws of the United States" a federal, rather than merely a state, crime.

But the Supreme Court overturned the conviction, saying in its opinion that the federal government did not have jurisdiction over state courts. In so doing, it refused to render a decision that would supersede the laws of individual states, thereby placing a huge roadblock in the way of civil rights.

In another example of federal judicial restraint, the *Slaughterhouse Cases* (1873),[3] Chief Justice Morrison R. Waite ruled that the constitutional right to assemble peaceably and the right to bear arms had evolved from *state* citizenship and thus were not subject to *federal* protection. As a result, the Supreme Court further limited the federal government in its powers to protect blacks.

The Court continued its practice of bowing to the powers of the states in the *Civil Rights Cases* (1883),[4] based upon the Civil Rights Act of 1875. In that act, Congress passed an order outlawing racial discrimination by operators of public accommodations and conveyances.

But the Court ruled that neither the Thirteenth nor the Fourteenth Amendment granted the federal government the authority to pass such sweeping laws, saying that Congress had the power to oversee the actions of individual states but did not have any power over the individual citizens of those states.

Along with similar Court findings in *United States v. Harris* (1883)[5] and *United States v. Reese* (1875),[6] the *Civil Rights Cases* effectively stifled federal authority to protect recently freed black slaves.

But the Court's narrow approach to the protection of individual civil rights did not stop Congress from challenging what it saw as a clear violation of its intent to protect *all* American citizens, regardless of race or color. In *Plessy v. Ferguson* (1896),[7] the Court was faced with a Fourteenth Amendment challenge to a state statute that required railways to maintain separate carriages for whites and blacks. As it had done in the past, the Court leaned heavily toward supporting states' rights, saying that the Fourteenth Amendment "could not have been intended to abolish distinctions based on color, or to enforce social, as distinguished from political, equality."

The *Plessy* decision came in part from the unwritten but widely held belief among white Americans that blacks were inferior by nature, a concept shared even by the Supreme Court's Justice John Marshall Harlan. In his dissent in *Plessy*, Harlan explicitly noted that "[t]he white race deems itself to be the dominant race in this country. ... So, I doubt not, it will continue to be for all time, if it remains true to its great heritage, and holds fast to the principles of constitutional liberty." So long as the Court held such biased notions, it seemed unlikely that constitutional law and the best works of Congress could do much to change things.

It was beginning to appear that all the hard-won civil rights that Congress had secured following *Dred Scott* were slowly but steadily being worn away by, of all things, the US Supreme Court. Numerous cases brought before the Court merely strengthened the concept of the "separate but equal" doctrine that the Court had embraced for decades. Yes, according to the Constitution, all people are equal. But no, the Court insisted, they were not necessarily entitled to receive equal treatment under law. In *Gong Lum v. Rice* (1927),[8] the Court not only refused to force a state to allow a Chinese-American to attend classes with whites but also confirmed several lower court cases that applied the "separate but equal" doctrine to public education nationwide.

Clearly, something had gone wrong in Washington. The vision that Abraham Lincoln and Dred Scott had fostered of a nation undivided by racial differences was not the same vision that the US Supreme Court had held. Or, at least, so it seemed.

But by the early twentieth century, something remarkable happened. The Court began to change.

In several cases throughout the 1940s, the Court gave a wide interpretation of a federal statute prohibiting those who deprive persons of their civil rights "under color of law." In *Shelley v. Kraemer* (1948)[9] and *Barrows v. Jackson* (1953),[10] the Court refused to enforce private agreements not to sell real estate to blacks. Having held in *Buchanan v. Warley* (1917)[11] and *Harmon v. Tyler* (1927)[12] that the state could not directly restrict the right of blacks to live in particular neighborhoods, the Court in *Shelley* and *Barrows* had little difficulty declaring that racially restrictive covenants were unconstitutional.

In 1950, the Court moved once again closer toward invalidating state segregation and embracing universal civil rights. In *Sweatt v. Painter* (1950),[13] it concluded that a law school for blacks was not "functionally equivalent" to a school for whites, because by its nature it excluded most of those with whom black graduates would have to deal for the rest of their professional lives. And in *McLaurin v. Oklahoma State Regents for Higher Education* (1950),[14] the Court found unconstitutional a program in which blacks could attend the same graduate schools as whites but were kept physically segregated from their white counterparts.

Although the Court throughout the early twentieth century had been moving gradually toward striking down the "separate but equal" doctrine that had governed America since *Dred Scott*, it would take an extraordinary new chief justice to bring the Court out of the darkness and into a new era of enlightened judiciary.

The Warren Era

In 1954, under the leadership of newly appointed Chief Justice Earl Warren, the US Supreme Court became increasingly sensitive to its slowly evolving role of protecting the civil rights of minority Americans. One of its earliest campaigns began with the landmark decisions in *Brown v. Board of Education of Topeka* (1954)[15] and its companion case, *Bolling v. Sharpe* (1954).[16] But unlike previous cases dealing with segregation within education, *Brown* tackled head-on the legitimacy of the separate-but-equal doctrine.

Focusing on the critical role that education plays in human development, the Court ruled that the maintenance of government-ordered segregated schools was inconsistent with the Fourteenth Amendment's equal protection clause. "We conclude," Warren wrote in his decision, "that in the field of public education the doctrine of 'separate but equal' has no place. Separate educational facilities are inherently unequal."

In so finding, the Court, in sharp contrast to both *Dred Scott* and *Plessy*, pointed to the stigma placed upon blacks by America's mostly segregated school system. It made clear the Court's determination to invalidate all state-imposed programs of racial bias and segregation.

Interestingly, although the Court could have struck down the idea that the equal protection clause entitled the federal government to legislate matters *directly* involving states' activities, it did not. Instead, it dramatically expanded what the Court's definition of states' rights was so that, even in the case of individual activities, such as operating a shoeshine stand in a public building, the Court considered that operation to be a state matter for constitutional purposes. By opening up the interpretation of the equal protection clause to include individual activities, the Warren Court had greatly expanded the scope of the Fourteenth Amendment's civil rights protections.

Brown was the Warren Court's first successful foray into the civil rights arena, but it would not be its last. The Court would soon uphold and help define the Civil Rights Act and the Voting Rights Act, which Congress had passed in 1964 and 1965 respectively, both aimed at ending racial discrimination.

Predictably, opponents of both statutes argued that Congress had exceeded the authority granted to it under the constitution when drafting the laws. The Supreme Court uniformly rejected the challenges.

At times, the Court was forced to rely on its own creative inventiveness in order to withstand pressure from opponents of civil rights, as it did when the Civil Rights Act's Title II, which prohibited discrimination in providing public accommodations, was challenged. In upholding the statute, the Court in *Heart of Atlanta Motel, Inc. v. United States* (1964)[17] and *Katzenbach v. McClung* (1964)[18] focused on the power of Congress to regulate interstate commerce. Although that regulatory power is most often thought of in terms of laws affecting the movement of real goods around the country (coffee, soy beans, oil, and so forth), the Court expanded the definition of interstate commerce to embrace the notion that racial discrimination had an adverse effect on the free movement of not only goods but also people. Thus, it concluded, Congress had a *right* under the interstate commerce laws to regulate those laws that the lower courts had a responsibility to uphold. And still one more doorway leading back to *Dred Scott* had been opened.

More recently, the US Supreme Court has found itself challenged to consider more exotic and less obvious forms of civil rights violations. In *Regents of the University of California v. Bakke* (1978),[19] the Court imposed limitations on affirmative action to ensure that providing greater opportunities for minorities did not come at the expense of fewer rights for the majority. Affirmative action—or allowing minorities special privileges in applying for college in order to make right years of "wrongdoing"—was unfair if it lead to reverse discrimination, or discrimination against whites. The case involved the University of California Davis School of Medicine and Allan Bakke, a white applicant who was rejected twice even though minority applicants who had significantly lower scores than he had were admitted. A closely divided Court ruled that, while race *was* a legitimate factor in school admissions, the use of rigid quotas (reverse discrimination) was not permissible.

In 2003, *Grutter v. Bollinger*[20] upheld the University of Michigan Law School's consideration of race and ethnicity in admissions. In her majority opinion, Justice Sandra Day O'Connor said that the law school used a "highly individualized, holistic review of each applicant's file." Race, she said, was not used in a "mechanical way." Therefore, the university's program was consistent with the requirement of "individualized consideration" set in the 1978 *Bakke* case.

"In order to cultivate a set of leaders with legitimacy in the eyes of the citizenry," she wrote in her opinion, "it is necessary that the path to leadership be visibly open to talented and qualified individuals of every race and ethnicity." In its findings, however, the Court ruled that the University of Michigan's undergraduate admissions system (as opposed to its law school's system), which awarded twenty points to black, Hispanic, and American Indian applicants, was "non-individualized, mechanical," and thus unconstitutional.

CHAPTER 10
Civil Rights Since *Dred Scott*

F rom the time of Dred Scott to the present, few issues visiting the US Supreme Court have loomed so large or weighed so heavily as those involving civil rights. The case of *Dred Scott v. Sandford* was the first such case of its time. It was the first time the issue of slavery, citizenship, and civil rights had risen to a challenge of such magnitude in the United States that it could no longer be ignored. But it would not be the last time.

Since *Dred Scott,* numerous cases have come before the Court, no one less or more important than the others (although some are more noteworthy or even notorious than the rest). Peering back through the looking glass of time from the 2003 case of *Grutter v. Bollinger* to the present, a wide range of civil rights cases stare back.

In January, 2009, in *Ricci v. DeStefano,* eighteen plaintiffs (seventeen white and one Hispanic) argued before the Supreme Court that results of the 2003 lieutenant and captain exams in the City of New Haven, Connecticut, were thrown out when the city realized that relatively few black firefighters had qualified for advancement. The city claimed they threw out the results because it feared liability under a statute for issuing tests that discriminated against minority firefighters. The eighteen plaintiffs claimed that they were victims of *reverse discrimination* under Title VII of the Civil Rights Act of 1964. The Supreme Court ruled 5-4 in favor of the firefighters, saying New Haven's "action in discarding the tests was a violation of Title VII." As a result, New Haven reinstated the examination results and promoted fourteen of the twenty firefighters within months of the decision. The city settled the lawsuit by paying $2 million to the firefighter plaintiffs; each promotable individual received three years of "service time" toward his pension; and the city paid their attorney $3 million in fees and costs.[1]

On June 25, 2013, in *Shelby County v. Holder,* the Supreme Court struck down Section 4 of the Voting Rights Act, which established a formula for Congress to use to determine if a state or voting jurisdiction requires prior approval before changing its voting laws. The Court ruled by a 5-4 vote that Section 4(b) was unconstitutional because the coverage formula was based on data over forty years old, making it no longer responsive to current needs and therefore an impermissible burden on the constitutional principles of federalism and equal sovereignty of the states.[2] Chief Justice John Roberts said the formula Congress used was written in 1965 and had long since grown outdated.

"While any racial discrimination in voting is too much," Roberts said, "Congress must ensure that the legislation it passes to remedy that problem speaks to current conditions."

In a strongly worded dissent, Justice Ruth Bader Ginsburg said, "Hubris is a fit word for today's demolition of the V. R. A. [Voting Rights Act]."

Meanwhile, June 2013's *Arizona v. Inter Tribal Council of Arizona*, seemed to bend over backwards to ensure that every US citizen had not only the right but also the *opportunity* to vote. The Court overturned an existing Arizona law that had required that voter registration applications not accompanied by proof of citizenship be disallowed. Instead, it referred Arizona state officials to the federal National Voter Registration Act.[3]

Then, also in 2013, in the case of *United States v. Windsor*, the Court struck down Section 3 of the Defense of Marriage Act, which defined marriage as applying *only* to heterosexual couples for purposes of federal law, saying that the law was a violation of the Fifth Amendment and opening the door to legalizing same-sex marriages.[4] On the very same day, the Court ruled on marriage equality at the state level in *Hollingsworth v. Perry*. While overturning a California ballot measure to end same-sex marriages, the Supreme Court upheld the concept that same-sex marriages are legal, and they resumed in the state of California.[5]

In that same year, in *Fisher v. University of Texas*, a challenge to the university's use of race in undergraduate admissions, the Court reinforced the application of strict scrutiny in reviewing such practices, requiring a university to ensure such programs are "narrowly tailored." No longer could a state use a universal set of rules to apply equally to different people. But following an appeal, on June 29, 2015, the Supreme Court announced that they would hear another challenge to University of Texas at Austin's admissions policy. The case was assigned docket number 14-981 and oral arguments were heard on December 9. The Court upheld UT Austin's admissions policy.[6]

In 2014, in *Burwell v. Hobby Lobby Stores, Inc.*, the Supreme Court held that the Religious Freedom Restoration Act of 1993 allows a closely held corporation to deny its employees contraceptive healthcare coverage based on the employer's religious objections.[7]

This landmark decision allowed closely held, for-profit corporations to be exempt from a law its owners religiously object to if there is a less restrictive means of furthering the law's interest. It is the first time that the Court has recognized a for-profit corporation's claim of religious belief, but it is limited to *closely held* corporations. The decision is an interpretation of the Religious Freedom Restoration Act (RFRA) and does not address whether such corporations are protected by the free exercise of religion clause of the First Amendment of the Constitution.

For such companies, the Court's majority directly struck down by a 5-4 vote the contraceptive mandate, a regulation adopted by the US Department of Health and Human Services (HHS) under the Affordable Care Act (ACA).

The ACA required employers to cover certain contraceptives for their female employees.

The ruling could have widespread impact, allowing corporations to claim religious exemptions from federal laws.

Also in 2014, in *Schuette v. Coalition to Defend Affirmative Action*, the Court upheld Michigan's state constitutional amendment prohibiting state universities from considering race as part of its admissions process.[8]

In an April 2014 ruling cheered by voting-rights advocates, Judge Lynn Adelman of the Federal District Court in Milwaukee struck down a 2011 Wisconsin law requiring voters to produce a state photo ID at polls, saying the law violated both the Fourteenth Amendment's equal protection clause and Section 2 of the Voting Rights Act, which prohibits voting procedures that discriminate on the basis of race or color.

"Blacks and Latinos in Wisconsin are disproportionately likely to live in poverty," Adelman wrote in his ninety-page opinion.

Individuals who live in poverty are less likely to drive or participate in other activities for which a photo ID may be required (such as banking, air travel, and international travel) and so they obtain fewer benefits from possession of a photo ID than do individuals who can afford to participate in these activities.

Adelman added, "Virtually no voter impersonation occurs in Wisconsin, and it is exceedingly unlikely that voter impersonation will become a problem in Wisconsin in the foreseeable future." The law, however, was restored in September 2014 by the US Court of Appeals for the Seventh Circuit. In October, the Supreme Court stepped in and blocked the law, saying changing the law weeks before election day would create confusion for poll workers and voters.[9]

The Court also ruled in 2015's *Young v. UPS* that employers accommodating non-pregnant workers with injuries or disabilities, but excluding pregnant workers, were in violation of the Pregnancy Discrimination Act, thus making available equal rights to pregnant workers.[10]

In 2015, in *King v. Burwell,* the Supreme Court rejected a challenge to the Affordable Care Act that would have eliminated subsidies for people who purchased health insurance through the federal exchanges in thirty-four states. In a 5-4 decision, the Court upheld the individual mandate requiring most Americans to enroll in health insurance coverage.

However, the Court ruled as unconstitutional the provision in the law that threatened loss of existing Medicaid funds for states that did not participate in the expansion. Congress, it said, could offer additional funds under the Affordable Care Act to states that choose to expand Medicaid eligibility, but they could not withhold *existing* federal funds for Medicaid from states that do not participate in the expansion.[11]

Also in 2015, in *Obergefell v. Hodges,* the Court struck down state bans on same-sex marriage, thereby granting the constitutional right to marry to LGBT Americans throughout the country.[12]

And so the cases continue to unfold. While *Dred Scott* may have been a pioneering case in civil rights for America, it was far from the *only* case with far-reaching consequences throughout society.

Where will the gavel fall on the next major civil rights case? To the right or to the left of the American political scene? And which justices will be on the Court at the time to make that decision?

Only time will answer those questions. Time, and the future rulings of the US Supreme Court. US Supreme Court legal decisions are an ongoing and evolutionary fact of life. They are not written in stone but rather interpreted in the light of an ever-changing society.

Today, the Court continues to be challenged to rule upon cases concerning the civil rights of minorities, many of those cases less obvious than that of a Negro slave petitioning for his freedom back in 1857. Those supporters of civil rights who advocate righting the wrongs of *Dred Scott* and, later, *Plessy* rely upon the Court's gradually expanding definition of minority groups entitled to federal protection under the constitution.

As a result of *Dred Scott* and its aftermath, minorities across the board have had protections granted to them by the legislature and upheld by the Supreme Court. In *West Coast Hotel Company v. Parrish* (1937), the Court upheld minimum wages for women,[13] and in *Roe v. Wade* (1973), it confirmed a woman's right to abortion.[14]

In addition, the Court has decided on matters of civil rights affecting gay men and women, the physically and mentally handicapped, and children. In fact, wherever a minority exists, the Court either has ruled on that group's rights or likely will be petitioned to do so in the near future.

By its very nature, a minority group does not have the power, the financial resources, or the political force often necessary to secure its own protection. For minority persons everywhere, Congress has passed laws, and the Supreme Court has acted to uphold them, all in the name of protecting the minority's civil rights.

And it all began with a man named Dred Scott more than 150 years ago. He had the courage and the conviction of his beliefs to pursue his right to freedom, even after the lower courts had stripped him of it. It took President Abraham Lincoln's Emancipation Proclamation, a brutal Civil War, and the passage of the Reconstruction Amendments to restore that freedom to him.

Since then, an enlightened US Supreme Court has denounced the horrific decision of Chief Justice Roger Taney and his Court and reaffirmed the rights of minorities everywhere so that those who are suffering under inequality and injustice could be made whole again.

Today, Americans—of every color and race, of every religious, political, social, and sexual orientation—are free to enjoy the same inalienable rights. And they all have Dred Scott to thank.

Questions to Consider

1. Who was Dred Scott?

2. Where was Dred Scott born?

3. Why did Dred Scott claim he was free?

4. Summarize the basic argument made by Dred Scott's lawyers in the Missouri Circuit Court (the state court) and explain why Scott had reason to believe he would win his case.

5. How did the bitter political climate of the day affect Dred Scott's chances of winning his case?

6. What did the Court decide regarding Dred Scott's right to sue in federal court?

7. Why was the *Dred Scott* decision so important to the issue of slavery in the United States?

8. How was Dred Scott finally freed from slavery?

Primary Source Documents

In the Court's 7-2 decision rejecting Dred Scott's plea for freedom, Chief Justice Roger Taney laid the groundwork for the Court's action, explaining in his majority opinion why Dred Scott was not entitled to be free.

"Upon the whole, therefore," Taney wrote at the conclusion of his lengthy opinion, "it is the judgment of this Court, that it appears by the record before us that the plaintiff in error is not a citizen of Missouri, in the sense in which that word is used in the Constitution; and that the Circuit Court of the United States, for that reason, had no jurisdiction in the case, and could give no judgment in it. Its judgment for the defendant must, consequently, be reversed, and a mandate issued, directing the suit to be dismissed for want of jurisdiction."

Justice Wayne, in concurring with Taney, wrote, "I will not argue a point already so fully discussed. I have every confidence in the opinion of the Court upon the point of jurisdiction, and do not allow myself to doubt that the error of a contrary conclusion will be fully understood by all who shall read the argument of the Chief Justice.

I have already said that the opinion of the Court has my unqualified assent."

Justices Nelson and Grier concurred, writing short opinions in support of Taney. Meanwhile, Justice Daniel, in an opinion only somewhat shorter than the several thousand words written by Taney, concurred, with some minor disagreements with the majority opinion:

"In conclusion, my opinion is, that the decision of the Circuit Court, upon the law arising upon the several pleas in bar, is correct, but that it is erroneous in having sustained the demurrer to the plea in abatement of the jurisdiction; that for this error the decision of the Circuit Court should be reversed, and the cause remanded to that Court, with instructions to abate the action, for the reason set forth and pleaded in the plea in abatement."

Justices Campbell and Catron wrote similarly lengthy concurring opinions.

In *dissension* of the majority opinion, Justice McLean, in several thousand words, concluded that the Supreme Court of the State of Missouri was incorrect in saying that Dred Scott had no standing to sue for his freedom:

"The Supreme Court of Missouri refused to notice the act of Congress or the Constitution of Illinois, under which Dred Scott, his wife and children, claimed that they are entitled to freedom.

This being rejected by the Missouri Court, there was no case before it, or least it was a case with only one side. And this is the case which, in the opinion of this Court, we are bound to follow. The Missouri Court disregards the express provisions of an act of Congress and the Constitution of a sovereign State, both of which laws for twenty-eight years it had not only regarded, but carried into effect."

Similarly dissenting, Justice Curtis wrote for the minority a lengthy, detailed, and withering opinion concluding that the Supreme Court should have reversed the decision of the Circuit Court of the United States and remanded the case back for a new trial:

"I have expressed [in my dissent] my opinion, and the reasons therefor, at far greater length than I could have wished, upon the different questions on which I have found it necessary to pass, to arrive at a judgment on the case at bar. These questions are numerous, and the grave importance of some of them required me to exhibit fully the grounds of my opinion. I have touched no question which, in the view I have taken, it was not absolutely necessary for me to pass upon, to ascertain whether the judgment of the Circuit Court should stand or be reversed. I have avoided no question on which the validity of that judgment depends. To have done either more or less, would have been inconsistent with my views of my duty.

In my opinion, the judgment of the Circuit Court should be reversed, and the cause remanded for a new trial."

Chronology

1846–1847 Dred and Harriet Scott sue Mrs. Emerson for their freedom in the St. Louis Circuit Court. The circuit court rules in favor of Mrs. Emerson, dismissing the Scotts' case but allowing the Scotts to refile their suit.

1850 The jury in a second trial decides that the Scotts deserve to be free, based on their years of residence in the non-slave territories of Wisconsin and Illinois.

1852 Mrs. Emerson, not wanting to lose such valuable property, appeals the decision to the Missouri Supreme Court. The state supreme court overrules the circuit court decision and returns Scott to slavery.

1853–1854 Scott, supported by lawyers who oppose slavery, files suit in the US Federal Court in St. Louis. The defendant in this case is Mrs. Emerson's brother, John Sanford, who has assumed responsibility for John Emerson's estate. As a New York resident and technically beyond the jurisdiction of the Missouri State Court,

Scott's lawyers can only file a suit against Sanford in the federal judicial system. Again the court rules against Scott.

1856–1857 Scott and his lawyers appeal the case to the US Supreme Court. In *Scott v. Sandford*, the Court states that Scott should remain a slave because, as a slave, he is not a citizen of the United States and thus not eligible to bring suit in a federal court. He is personal property and therefore can never be free. The Court further declares unconstitutional the provision in the Missouri Compromise that permitted Congress to prohibit slavery in the territories.

Chapter Notes

Chapter 1. Dred and Harriet—Free or Slave?

1. *McCarthy's Weekly Reader,* February 2, 1856.

2. Ibid.

3. Herbert G. Gutman, *Who Built America?* (New York, NY: Pantheon Books, 1989), p. 379.

4. John A. Bryan, "The Blow Family and Their Slave Dred Scott," *Missouri Historical Society Bulletin IV,* July 1948, pp. 223–225; Estate of Peter Blow, Probate Court Records, no. 976, St. Louis.

5. *St. Louis Daily Evening News,* May 26, 1857.

6. John H. Hauberg, "U.S. Army Surgeons at Fort Armstrong," *Journal of the Illinois State Historical Society 24,* January 1932, p. 617.

7. Ibid., p. 619.

8. Emerson file, National Archives and Records Administration, Washington, DC.

9. Deposition of Miles H. Clark, May 13, 1847, in *Dred Scott v. Sanford*, Circuit Court of St. Louis County, St. Louis, MO.

10. Don E. Fehrenbacher, *The Dred Scott Case: Its Significance in American Law and Politics* (New York, NY: Oxford University Press, 1978), p. 244.

11. Ibid., p. 245.

12. Alfred Brunson, *A Western Pioneer* (Cincinnati, OH: Hitchcock & Walden, 1873–1879), vol. 2, p. 125.

13. Dred Scott Collection, Missouri Historical Society, St. Louis, MO.

Chapter 2. A History of Slavery

1. Herbert G. Gutman, *Who Built America?* (New York, NY: Pantheon Books, 1989), p. 365.

2. Ibid., pp. 365–366.

3. Ibid., p. 385.

Chapter 3. Suing for Freedom

1. Frederick Trevor Hill, *Decisive Battles of the Law* (New York, NY: Fred B. Rothman and Co., 1907), pp. 117–118.

2. *St. Louis Evening News*, April 3, 1857; *St. Louis Globe Democrat*, January 10, 1886.

3. J. Hugo Grimm to Charles Van Ravenswaay, October 29, 1946, citing 1867 records of Calvary Cemetery, Dred Scott Collection, Missouri Historical Society, St. Louis, MO.

4. Walter Ehrlich, *They Have No Rights: Dred Scott's Struggle for Freedom* (Westport, CT: Greenwood Press, 1979), p. 47.

5. *Emerson v. Harriet Scott* (of color); *Emerson v. Dred Scott* (of color), 11 Missouri 413 (1848).

6. *Dred Scott v. Emerson*, 15 Missouri 576, pp. 582–587.

7. Ibid.

8. Bond of Taylor Blow, November 2, 1853, and Writ of Summons, November 2, 1853, in *Dred Scott v. Sanford*, no. 692, US Circuit Court at St. Louis.

Chapter 4. To the Supreme Court

1. *St. Louis Morning Herald*, "Interesting Law Case—A Question of Slavery," May 18, 1854.

2. Thomas Lawson, *State Trials*, XIII, pp. 243–245.

3. Ray Allen Billington, *Westward Expansion: A History of the American Frontier* (New York, NY: Macmillan Co., 1974), pp. 274–275.

4. Kenneth C. Davis, *Don't Know Much About History* (New York, NY: Avon Books, 1990), pp. 154–156.

5. *Scott v. Sandford*, 60 U.S. 393 (1856).

6. *St. Louis Daily Missouri Democrat*, February 25, 1856.

7. *Washington Star*, February 13, 1856, as reported in the *New York Daily Tribune*, February 15, 1856.

8. Ibid.

9. George Brown Tindall, *America: A Narrative History* (New York, NY: W. W. Norton and Co., 1984), p. 600.

10. Don E. Fehrenbacher, *The Dred Scott Case: Its Significance in American Law and Politics* (New York, NY: Oxford University Press, 1978), pp. 300–304.

11. Ibid.

12. *Daily Missouri Democrat*, February 25, 1856.

13. *New York Daily Tribune*, February 18, 1856.

14. *Daily Missouri Republican*, February 21, 1856.

15. David M. Potter, *The Impending Crisis, 1848–1861* (New York, NY: Harper and Row, 1976), p. 276.

16. Walter Ehrlich, *They Have No Rights: Dred Scott's Struggle for Freedom* (Westport, CT: Greenwood Press, 1979), p. 102.

17. Ibid., p. 104.

Chapter 5. To Court Again

1. Walter Ehrlich, *They Have No Rights: Dred Scott's Struggle for Freedom* (Westport, CT: Greenwood Press, 1979), p. 109.

Chapter 6. The Court's Decision

1. Don E. Fehrenbacher, *The Dred Scott Case: Its Significance in American Law and Politics* (New York, NY: Oxford University Press, 1978), p. 308.

2. Ibid.

3. Ibid., pp. 316–319.

4. Ibid., p. 319.

5. Frank B. Latham, *The Dred Scott Decision: March 6, 1857* (New York, NY: Franklin Watts, 1968), p. 32.

Chapter 7. After *Dred Scott*

1. Herbert G. Gutman, *Who Built America?* (New York, NY: Pantheon Books, 1989), p. 404.

2. Ibid.

3. Ibid., pp. 404–405.

4. Don E. Fehrenbacher, *The Dred Scott Case: Its Significance in American Law and Politics* (New York, NY: Oxford University Press, 1978), pp. 420–421.

5. *New York Tribune,* March 17, 1857.

6. Gutman, pp. 407–409.

7. Frank B. Latham, *The Dred Scott Decision: March 6, 1857* (New York, NY: Franklin Watts, 1968), p. 39.

8. David Wallechinsky and Irving Wallace, *The People's Almanac* (Garden City, NY: Doubleday and Co., 1975), p. 285.

9. Kenneth C. Davis, *Don't Know Much About History* (New York, NY: Avon Books, 1990), p. 160.

10. Gutman, p. 407.

11. Ibid., p. 422.

12. Davis, pp. 158–161.

13. George Brown Tindall, *America: A Narrative History* (New York, NY: W. W. Norton and Co., 1984), p. 619.

14. Ibid., p. 613.

15. Davis, p. 165.

Chapter 8. Abraham Lincoln Acts

1. Jeffery A. Smith, *War and Press Freedom* (New York, NY: Oxford University Press, 1999), p. 111.

2. *The Columbia Encyclopedia*, 6th edition, s. v. "Ex parte Merryman," *Encyclopedia.com*, www.encyclopedia.com/doc/1E1-Merryman.html.

3. *The Oxford Companion to American Military History*, s. v. "Merryman, Ex Parte," by John Whiteclay Chambers II, *Encyclopedia.com*, www.encyclopedia.com/doc/1O126-MerrymanExParte.html.

4. Ibid.

5. Alexander M. Bickel, *The Supreme Court and the Idea of Progress* (New York, NY: Macmillan Co., 1970), p. 41.

Chapter 9. The Reconstruction Years

1. Ruth Ann Whiteside, "Justice Joseph Bradley and the Reconstruction Amendments" (doctor of philosophy thesis, Rice University, 1981), scholarship.rice.edu/handle/1911/15658.

2. *United States v. Cruikshank*, 92 U.S. 542 (1875).

3. *Slaughterhouse Cases*, 83 U.S. 36 (1872).

4. *Civil Rights Cases*, 109 U.S. 3 (1883).

5. *United States v. Harris*, 106 U.S. 629 (1883).

6. *United States v. Reese*, 92 U.S. 214 (1875).

7. *Plessy v. Ferguson*, 163 U.S. 537 (1896).

8. *Gong Lum v. Rice*, 275 U.S. 78 (1927).

9. *Shelley v. Kraemer*, 334 U.S. 1 (1948).

10. *Barrows v. Jackson,* 346 U.S. 249 (1953).

11. *Buchanan v. Warley,* 235 U.S. 60 (1917).

12. *Harmon v. Tyler,* 273 U.S. 668 (1927).

13. *Sweatt v. Painter,* 339 U.S. 629 (1950).

14. *McLaurin v. Oklahoma State Regents for Higher Education,* 339 U.S. 637 (1950).

15. *Brown v. Board of Education of Topeka,* 347 U.S. 483 (1954).

16. *Bolling v. Sharpe,* 347 U.S. 497 (1954).

17. *Heart of Atlanta Motel, Inc. v. United States,* 379 U.S. 241 (1964).

18. *Katzenbach v. McClung,* 379 U.S. 294 (1964).

19. *Regents of University of California v. Bakke,* 438 U.S. 265 (1978).

20. *Grutter v. Bollinger,* 539 U.S. 306 (2003).

Chapter 10. Civil Rights Since *Dred Scott*

1. *Ricci v. DeStefano,* 557 U.S. 557 (2009).

2. *Shelby County v. Holder,* 570 U.S. ___(2013).

3. *Arizona v. Inter Tribal Council of Arizona,* 570 U.S. ___ (2013).

4. *United States v. Windsor,* 570 U.S. ___(2013).

5. *Hollingsworth v. Perry,* 570 U.S. ___ (2013).

6. *Fisher v. University of Texas,* 570 U.S. ___(2013).

7. *Burwell v. Hobby Lobby Stores, Inc.,* 573 U.S. ___(2014).

8. *Schuette v. Coalition to Defend Affirmative Action,* 572 U.S. ___ (2014).

9. Robert Barnes, "Supreme Court blocks Wisconsin voter ID law," *Washington Post,* October 9, 2014, www.washingtonpost.com/politics/courts_law/supreme-court-blocks-wisconsin-voter-id-law/2014/10/09/e52af8fe-4ff4-11e4-8c24-487e92bc997b_story.html?tid=a_inl.

10. *Young v. United Parcel Service, Inc.,* 575 U.S. ____(2015).

11. *King v. Burwell,* 576 U.S.____(2015).

12. *Obergefell v. Hodges,* 576 U.S. ____(2015).

13. *West Coast Hotel Company v. Parrish,* 300 U.S. 379 (1937).

14. *Roe v. Wade,* 410 U.S. 113 (1973).

Glossary

adjudication A court decision.

amendment A change to an existing agreement or rule.

bill A proposal that could become a law if it is passed by the House of Representatives and the Senate and is signed by the president.

dissenting opinion An opinion written by a judge or judges who disagree with the majority opinion.

evidence Something that is offered up as proof during a legal proceeding.

federal Having to do with the central (national) form of government, as opposed to a state or local government.

majority opinion A ruling supported by the majority of judges in a case.

petition A formal, official request.

precedent Prior legal decisions that establish a foundation for future decisions.

remand To send back to a lower court.

states' rights A political view that upholds the powers of the states as opposed to those of the federal government. In an extreme form, it argues that states should have veto power over acts of the central government.

unconstitutional law A law that the Supreme Court declares a violation of either the US constitution or state constitution.

United States Constitution The basic law forming the US government. It consists of seven articles and twenty-seven amendments.

United States Supreme Court A judicial body comprised of nine justices. As the highest court in the US, it holds final say over whether a law is constitutional.

Further Reading

Books

Finkelman, Paul. *Dred Scott v. Sandford: A Brief History with Documents*. New York, NY: Bedford/St. Martin's, 2016.

Hill, Frederick Trevor. *The Story of Dred Scott and the Dred Scott Decision*, Kindle Edition. Bayside, NY: A. J. Cornell Publications, 2013.

Jordan, Anne Devereaux, with Virginia Schomp. *Slavery and Resistance*. New York, NY: Marshall Cavendish/Benchmark Books, 2007.

Skog, Jason. *The Dred Scott Decision*. Minneapolis, MN: Compass Point Books, 2007.

Websites

Public Broadcasting System

www.pbs.org/wgbh/aia/part4/4p2932.html

A brief summary of the *Dred Scott* case.

The Dred Scott Heritage Foundation

www.thedredscottfoundation.org/

A site dedicated to the history and legacy of *Dred Scott.*

Oyez IIT Chicago-Kent College of Law

www.oyez.org/cases/1850-1900/60us393

Details about the *Dred Scott* case.

Index

Hamilton, Alexander, 28, 29, 30, 31, 72
Harlan, John Marshall, 92
Harmon v. Tyler, 93
Harpers Ferry, VA, 74
Harris, United States v., 91
Harvey, James E., 50
Heart of Atlanta Motel, Inc. v. United States, 96
Hollingsworth v. Perry, 101

J
Jackson, Andrew, 40
Johnson, Reverdy, 40, 45, 47, 48, 57
Jonathan Lemmon case, 47

K
Kansas-Nebraska Act, 40, 41, 49, 75
Katzenbach v. McClung, 96
King v. Burwell, 104

L
Lane, William Carr, 8
Lincoln, Abraham, 50, 76, 77, 78, 79, 80, 83, 84, 93, 106
Louisiana Purchase, 10, 19, 20, 40

M
McLaurin v. Oklahoma State Regents for Higher Education, 94
McLean, John, 50, 51, 64, 66

Merryman, Ex Parte, 84
Merryman, John, 84
Missouri Compromise, 6, 10, 21, 40, 41, 48, 49, 50, 55, 57, 58, 59, 62–64, 65, 66, 68
Missouri Supreme Court, 29, 30, 31
Murdoch, Francis B., 14

N
Napton, William B., 31
National Voter Registration Act, 101
Nelson, Samuel, 62, 64, 65, 66
Norris, Lyman D., 30
Northwest Ordinance, 9

O
Obergefell v. Hodges, 104
O'Connor, Sandra Day, 97

P
Parrish, West Coast Hotel Company v., 105
Passmore Williamson case, 47
permanent emancipation principle, 44, 45
plea in abatement, 58, 60, 62, 65
Plessy v. Ferguson, 92, 95, 105
popular sovereignty, 54
Potter, David M., 50
Pregnancy Discrimination Act, 104